# The Book of Humorous Legal Anecdotes

# The Book of Humorous Legal Anecdotes

SPRINGWOOD BOOKS
ASCOT, BERKSHIRE

First published 1988 by Springwood Books Limited
Springwood House, The Avenue, Ascot, Berkshire

Reprinted 1988

ISBN 0 86254 134 4

Designed by Denis Falkiner
Typeset by Inforum Ltd, Portsmouth
Printed and bound in Great Britain by
Butler & Tanner Ltd, Frome

# ACKNOWLEDGEMENTS

The idea of compiling a selection of the best legal stories came to me in 1986. So broad and traditional a subject as the law would yield a wealth of anecdotes, but how to reap such a harvest? Thousands of letters were dispatched to eminent members of the legal profession requesting material. The response from such a busy band of people was overwhelming. I am indebted to all who sent contributions. The book represents the cream of those anecdotes and my warmest thanks go to those contributors.

I should also like to join my publishers in thanking Butterworths for permission to quote copyright material from The All England Law Reports.

The cartoons of 'Bec' and 'Tak' compliment the anecdotes and my gratitude is extended to these two artists.

My joint editor, Peter Cochrane, was as ever an invaluable source of sound advice; I am very grateful to him. I would also like to thank those stalwart ladies Lesley Morris and Lynda Skinner of Springwood Books, whose inexhaustible patience and unfailing encouragement was a great deal more than I deserve.

T.R.F.

*To The Memory Of My Father*
*Kenneth John Foster*

# LIST OF CONTRIBUTORS

N.J. Adamson CB QC
The Rt Hon. Peter Archer
J.R. Atkinson
P.R. Ayers
W. Bealby
R. Benson
D.P. Blakey
J. Boyle
V.N. Brenner
A. Brewer
M.J. Burr
W.T. Chatterton
H.S. Cohen
His Honour Judge Gerald Coles QC
S. Corbishley
The Rt Hon. Sir Frederick Corfield QC
His Honour Judge Crowther QC
A.J. Curtis
His Honour Judge G. Darling
P.R. Davies
J.A. Eteson
K. Evans
N.J. Evans
T.R. Foster

A.I.F. Goldman
A. Goodman
R.A. Griffiths
M. Grundy
A. Hadik
K. Haggerty
R.G. Hamilton
J. Harvard
T.N. Heffron
K. Hill
J.A. Hitchen
T.D. Huckle
S.S. Jacobs
P.J. Kelson
M.C. Keogh
P.R. Leggatt
J. Lewis
M. Mansfield
His Honour Judge McCreery QC
Mr Justice Millett
M. Mitchell
I.H. Morton
C. Moss
P.A. Murden

C.J. Noel
A.R. Ostrin
W.D. Park
F.W. Parsons
T.G.W. Potts
R.G. Prince
S.A. Rayner
M. Read
H.J. Russell
J.F. Rutter
L. Skan
R. Spon-Smith
C.W. Stansfield
M. Steiner
D.S. Thomson
J.A. Trafford
J.D. Tunnicliffe
J.A. Turnbull
A. Turner
V. Usher
P.M. Walters
G.A.B. Ward
D. Weitzman QC
R. York QC

A juror-in-waiting approached the Clerk of Assize and enquired whether he might be discharged from service as his wife was expecting to be confined that afternoon. He was advised to make an application to the judge after the luncheon adjournment. After lunch the following exchange took place:

The Judge: 'I understand Mr . . . that you have an application to make. What is it?'
Mr . . .: 'My Lord, I wish to be released from service as my wife is expecting to conceive this afternoon.'
The Judge: 'I think you mean that she is expecting to be confined, but in either event you ought to be there. You are released.'

A man is travelling in the basket of a hot air balloon when the weather changes. The ground is covered by cloud and the wind blows unpredictably. When the cloud clears, he descends towards a man digging in a suburban garden. When he is within twenty feet of the ground, he calls to the digger, 'Where am I?'

'You are in the basket of a hot air balloon and approximately twenty feet from the ground,' is the reply.

'You' said the man in the basket, 'must be a barrister.'

'You are right,' says the digger. 'How do you know?'

'Because,' says the balloonist, 'what you say is wholly accurate, but of no practical value.'

Letter from wife's solicitors to husband:

Dear Sir,
We act for your Wife, who has instructed us to commence proceedings against you for nullity on the ground of non-consummation. We suggest that you instruct Solicitors, show them a copy of this letter and ask them to communicate with us.
Yours, etc.

Letter from husband to wife's solicitors:

Dear Sirs,
Thank you for your letter. I have forwarded a copy to Messrs X Y & Co., who will be acting for me, and who will no doubt be in communication with you. I should add that you are misinformed. My marriage was certainly consummated: we had intercourse on many occasions.
Yours etc.

Letter from husband's solicitors to wife's solicitors:

Dear Sirs,
We act for Mr Z, who has shown us a copy of your letter dated . . . Any proceedings will be strenuously contested. We suggest that you question your client again, as there seems to be no doubt that the marriage with our client was consummated. Indeed, we are instructed that intercourse took place frequently.
Yours etc.

Letter from wife's solicitors to husband's solicitors:

Dear Sirs,
Thank you for your letter dated . . .
In view of your remarks, we have closely questioned our client and are completely satisfied that the marriage was *not* consummated. Indeed, our client was not aware that the male member was capable of erection until she saw her Solicitors.
Yours etc.

'As God is my judge I am not guilty!' exclaimed the prisoner. The judge eyed him coldly. 'He's not, I am, you are,' he retorted.

When Lord Goddard was first a High Court Judge about 1936, an Irish defendant was sentenced to six years for armed robbery. The defendant threw a warden's cap at Goddard, saying 'Take that you old bugger'. The defendant appealed against the sentence. In due course the judgment of the Appeal Court was delivered by Mr Justice Rigby Smith. After increasing the length of sentence on the Irishman, the justice concluded 'And furthermore I understand you passed some observations on the character of our brother Goddard which upon profound reflection we find to be unfounded.'

*'I trust I am not boring your Lordship.'*

Some years ago, before the days of word processors, it was customary for a draft lease to be submitted by the landlord's solicitor to the purchaser's solicitor, and for the document to be returned by the purchaser's solicitor with amendments and marginal comments in red ink. The landlord's solicitor would then, in return, send it back to the tenant's solicitor for his further amendments and comments in green ink, and so the draft would go back and forth accumulating further colours and amendments, becoming more rainbow-like until it was finally approved and engrossed for signature.

The case in question concerned the grant of a new lease to an existing tenant at a rent that was substantially higher than before; it had been arrived at after some bargaining and protest on the part of the tenant. The clause in the draft lease relating to rent should have read '. . . yielding and paying the sum of Twenty Thousand Pounds per annum . . .'. Unfortunately, in typing the original draft, an 'n' was omitted from the word 'annum'. The draft lease was returned by the tenant's solicitor with his red ink amendments, including the insertion of the missing 'n' and with the marginal comment 'Our client is already paying through the nose – this is really going too far!'

A London County Court. Young Indian barrister presenting his first case. 'I will now call my first witness, Mr Bumbum Fricks.' Witness takes the stand. Counsel: 'Is your name Mr Bumbum Fricks?' Witness, indignant: 'No, my name is Mr Bumbum, I am a Fellow of Royal Institute of Chartered Surveyors.'

Judges are sometimes assisted in the correct determination of sentence by medical reports. Then again perhaps they are not:

'He demonstrates all the symptoms of incipient schizophrenia – but I am in two minds as to whether he is susceptible to treatment.'

Young and nervous counsel was presenting his first divorce case before a High Court judge, the petition alleging the husband's desertion. Throughout the opening address counsel described with his hands the upstairs of the former matrimonial home, especially the bedroom where the husband allegedly said that he was 'going back to Mother'. Counsel went on to describe the landing and, using his fingers, showed the husband's walk down the stairs, step by step and including the bend in the staircase. The judge was heard to say to his clerk 'Bloody good job it's not an adultery case'.

*'Mr Smithers . . . please do not lead the witness.'*

The following was said by a judge when sentencing a cheque fraudsman:

'I refer to your job as a manager of an art gallery. There are all sorts of art galleries as I know. I don't suppose that yours is like an art gallery in New York or Liverpool but no doubt it is concerned with varieties of fine art, with matters of sensitivity and with matters of beauty. Now beauty is related to truth; truth is related to morality; morality is related to honesty and it doesn't seem to me that your job is consistent with your present criminal career.'

A rather more experienced counsel engaged in a batch of undefended divorces realised that the solicitors had overpleaded one case, involving behaviour, in about 24 paragraphs and he was not going to get through the case in the usual four or five minutes. A hurried conference with the petitioner before the court sat confirmed counsel's view that, even if she were 'led' on dates, the client would undoubtedly confuse one incident of violence with another. In order to assist, counsel mimed each alleged act of the violent respondent. It worked well until the judge interrupted. 'Mr X, what are you going to do when you come to sub paragraph 18?' This alleged that the respondent had taken a running jump at the petitioner and kicked her up the bottom. 'I trust your Honour will feel that the petitioner and I have suffered enough injury before we get to that point,' said counsel suavely.

Moral: Never take your eyes off the judge.

A judge tried to explain to the jury that there were good reasons for a very late resumption after the luncheon adjournment:

'Judges are a bit like icebergs; a lot of them lie below the surface and there's a part of me which you don't see that only works in chambers.'

In the early 1950s a solicitor in a northern town concluded a successful prosecution and asked for costs against the accused. The clerk to the justices enquired what sum he had in mind. Rather tentatively the solicitor said, 'Five guineas, sir'. 'Good heavens', exclaimed the chairman of the bench, who was a local trade union official, 'that's more than a skilled man would get!'

Six pigeons were flying. Two were shot dead and fell to the ground. The other four continued in their flight. 'How many pigeons remained?' asked Professor Bloggs.

'Four' shouted the law student.

'You are wrong,' said the Professor. 'Two which fell to the ground remained.'

## *The Ambidextrous Sheriff*

The following judgment was delivered in the Natal Provincial Division court by Mr Justice Holmes:

'This is a whimsical case about a deputy sheriff who served a summons upon himself as defendant. As far as counsel are aware, this is the first time that it has happened in South Africa. The matter now comes before the Court as an application by the defendant for an order setting the service aside as irregular. The plaintiff issued summons against the deputy sheriff at Estcourt claiming £2,000 as damages for wrongful attachment. When the plaintiff's attorneys forwarded the summons to the deputy sheriff for service, he raised the question whether it would be regular for him to serve it on himself, and their reply was that this course would not be irregular, and indeed that if the summons were not served without further delay, the plaintiff would regard this as an irregularity. Thereupon the deputy sheriff served the summons on himself. He does not say how he accomplished this dextrous feat, save to aver modestly that he "went through the motions" – thereby no doubt letting his left hand know what his right hand was doing. For this nimble service he charged the plaintiff a fee of 10s. 7d, which included cost of living allowance – an ambidextrous sheriff must live. The return of service indicates that he explained to himself the "nature and exigency of the summons". Doubtless this involved a little autosuggestion! Thereafter, he was prudent enough to enter appearance to defend. But the arrival of the declaration apparently caused him to have some misgivings, and he now applies, as defendant, for the service to be set aside as irregular. His right hand however has not lost its cunning, for he seeks to turn the irregularity to his advantage with a tactical prayer that the plaintiff be ordered to pay the costs of this application before reserving the summons, upon the ground that the plaintiff is a man of straw – a prayer which, if granted, might have the effect of preventing him from bringing his case before the Court.

Well now what is the Court to do about this drollery?

It seems to me obvious that it is irregular for a sheriff or a deputy sheriff to serve a summons upon himself. In the present case, either the plaintiff or the deputy sheriff could have asked the sheriff to appoint a temporary deputy for the purpose of serving the summons. But the fact that I hold that the service in this case was irregular does not necessarily mean that it should be set aside.

In the present case, looking at the facts on the ground, the position is that the defendant did receive the summons and understand the nature and exigency thereof and enter appearance, and he has suffered no prejudice, and he can plead to the declaration; while to set aside the service now would involve the plaintiff in needless expense and repetition of procedural steps. In all these circumstances it seems to me that plain justice between man and man requires that the irregularity be condoned and the application dismissed. There will be no order as to costs because both sides were partly responsible for the irregularity of which the applicant complains.

*Acknowledgement and undertaking*

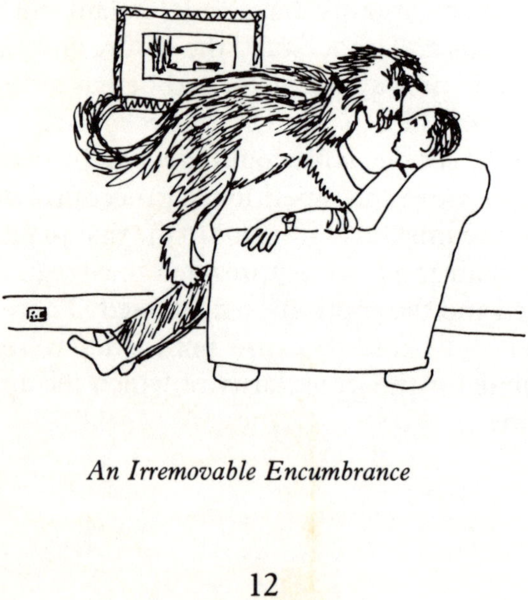

*An Irremovable Encumbrance*

Prosecuting counsel, in a Welsh trial, was just opening the case when it was realized that the jury numbered thirteen. The confusion was noticed when the thirteenth juror could not sit comfortably on the rear bench. The reason was the fact that there were ten jurors called Evans in the box.

Leeds Magistrates' Court (1984): solicitor addressing magistrates and putting forward as surety for bail the defendant's father who had recently been involved in an accident.

'I can identify my client's father – he's the man at the back of the court holding his crutch.'

A well known solicitor advocate, arriving at the last minute in the court of an equally well known metropolitan magistrate, found the solicitors' bench full apart from one small space in the middle. Hc also noticed that all the solicitors there had ethnic origins outside the United Kingdom.

He managed to reach the small space just before the magistrate entered and bowed to the court, nodding recognition to the late arrival. As soon as he sat down the magistrate wrote a note and handed it to the clerk, who passed it to the solicitor. It said simply, 'Dr Livingstone, I presume'.

*'Gold is up two points but paper doesn't seem to be moving at all.'*

## *The Page Three Girl*

Several years ago I acted for an unfortunate girl who worked for a large electrical concern in the Greater Manchester area, testing fluorescent tubes.

One of the tubes exploded and she was showered with hot glass, pieces of which lodged under her brassiere, since she was wearing an open necked T-shirt.

As a result, a claim was made against her employers' insurance company, not known at the time for their humour or indeed their human approach to these matters. Certainly they used to be one of the more difficult insurance companies to deal with.

As a result of the accident, my client was left with a small red scar on her left breast. As all lawyers in personal injury work know, scarring on a woman is obviously a cosmetic disability but all scarring is certainly subjective when it comes to valuing the claim. Lo and behold, the client supplied me with colour photographs of her injuries in a 'Page Three' pose. I sent them to the insurance company to evaluate the extent of the cosmetic scarring from the burn and value the claim. In view of the reputation of this particular insurance company, it came as a great surprise to me when they replied that they felt the injury was worth £750, but as long as they could keep the photographs they would be willing to pay £1000!

My client was delighted to accept the offer.

*Further and Better Particulars*

*Discovery and Inspection*

*Beats as it sweeps as it . . .*

The case concerned a vacuum cleaner. The issue was whether a public house landlady had put it to domestic or commercial use. Counsel had subtly tried to gather information but finally had to put the question point-blank:

'Mrs Smythe, I will not beat around the bush any more, I will ask you the question straight: did you use the vacuum cleaner for cleaning the public parts of your public house only, or did you use it to clean your private parts also?'

Poor Mrs Smythe looked most put out, not to say shocked, as she shyly said:

'Oh no, not to clean my private parts, no never . . .'

During a case being heard at Doncaster Magistrates Court a local solicitor was mitigating for a young man who had pleaded guilty to an assault, as a result of which assault the complainant had allegedly suffered a broken leg. Part of the mitigation went 'Your Worships, it wasn't a bad break, it may well have been a hairline fracture – if it was a fracture at all. It may just have been a crack.'

Some years ago I was acting for a purchaser in a conveyancing transaction from two Jewish gentlemen for whom Mr Ben Hamilton, the Merthyr County Borough Coroner, and a well known character in Merthyr Tydfil, was acting. On examining the title deeds I found that the last conveyance was to the present two vendors and a Mr Benjamine Schwartz, whom I assume had died. On submitting my requisition on title to Mr Hamilton I raised a requisition which said 'Please supply evidence of the death of Benjamine Schwartz' and expected to receive from Mr Hamilton a copy death certificate. Mr Hamilton's reply to the requisition was 'I attended his funeral'.

During the course of a plea of mitigation after his client had been convicted, a counsel said:

'The defendant went up the alleyway intending to urinate and did so on my instructions.'

Some advocates display unconscious courage in their choice of argument. Two orthodox Jewish families were disputing a relative's will. They submitted their dispute to the court of the Chief Rabbi, and instructed solicitors to appear on their behalf. One solicitor, later describing to his colleagues what happened, explained that he had been anxious to get the court to apply English, rather than Rabbinical, law. The Rabbis had asked him what authority he had for the proposition that they should apply the secular and not the religious law. 'I told them,' he said 'that they should render unto Caesar the things which were Caesar's.'

*'Court 5? This is Rubber Duck in Court 3 . . . I have a motion for you . . .'*

The case concerned a restaurant in the heart of London's Chinatown. All the witnesses were Chinese. The question was whether a document, which appeared to create a tenancy agreement, was intended to be legally binding, or was merely an informal and non-binding arrangement between friends. Cross-examining the party who claimed to be the tenant, counsel asked:

'Was this document intended to be enforceable?'

'Oh yes,' the witness replied.

And three heavies, sitting at the back of the court, solemnly nodded their agreement.

Judge Benedict pronounced a famous sentence upon the convicted murderer, Jose Maria Martin, in the Taos County District Court, New Mexico. The state of facts proved during the trial showed utmost brutality on the part of the murderer and there were no mitigating circumstances.

'Jose Maria Martin, stand up: Jose Maria Martin, you have been indicted, tried and convicted by a jury of your countrymen of the crime of murder, and the court is now about to pass upon you the dread sentence of the law. As a usual thing, Jose Maria Martin, it is a painful duty for the judge of a court of justice to pronounce upon a human being the sentence of death. There is something horrible about it, and the mind of the court naturally revolts from the performance of such a duty. Happily, however, your case is relieved of all such unpleasant features and the court takes positive delight in sentencing you to death!

'You are a young man, Jose Maria Martin – apparently of good physical condition and robust health. Ordinarily, you might have looked forward to many years of life, and the court has no doubt you had expected to die at a ripe old age; but you are about to be cut off in consequence of your own act. Jose Maria Martin, it is now spring-time. In a little while the grass will be springing up green in these beautiful valleys, and on these broad mesas and mountainside flowers will be blooming: birds will be singing their sweet carols, and nature will be putting on her most gorgeous and her most attractive robes, and life will be pleasant and men will want to stay, but none of this for you, Jose Maria Martin. The flowers will not bloom for you, Jose Maria Martin; the birds will not carol for you, Jose Maria Martin; when these things come to gladden the senses of men, you will be occupying a space of about six by two beneath the sod, and the green grass and those beautiful flowers will be growing above your lowly head.

'The sentence of the court is that you be taken from this place to the county jail, that you be kept there safely and securely confined, in the custody of the sheriff until the day appointed for your execution. (Be very careful, Mr Sheriff, that he have no opportunity to escape and that you have him at the appointed place at the appointed time.) That you be so kept, Jose Maria Martin, until –

'Mr Clerk, on what day of the month does Friday, about two weeks from this time come? March Twenty-second your Honour.

'Very well, until Friday the twenty-second of March, when you will be taken by the sheriff from your place of confinement to some safe and convenient spot within the county – (That is in your discretion, Mr Sheriff, you are only confined to the limits of this county) – and that you be there hanged by the neck until you are dead and the court was about to add, Jose Maria Martin, 'May God have mercy on your soul', but the court will not assume the responsibility of asking an allwise providence to do that which a jury of your peers has refused to do. The Lord will not have mercy on your soul! However, if you affect any religious belief, or are connected with any religious organisation, it might be well for you to send for your priest or your minister and get from him such consolation as you can; but the court advises you to place no reliance upon anything of that kind!

Mr Sheriff, remove the prisoner.'

The sequel to the story is that Martin in all probability did see the green grass and beautiful flowers of the spring. He escaped and was never heard of or seen again to answer to the law.

At a lecture for lawyers on unsatisfactory aspects of the law of rape, an experienced old solicitor, who tended to impatience when academic analysis was being preferred to applied commonsense, listened with mounting exasperation to a long-winded exposition of the problems of corroboration, and finally interrupted the speaker by saying, 'If I was accused of rape at my time of life I should feel so flattered that I should plead guilty.'

In a recent robbery case the defence counsel is cross-examining the main witness for the prosecution who purports to identify the robber. Counsel is attempting to get the witness to describe the robber without being influenced by the appearance of the defendant in the dock. Counsel therefore asks the witness to turn towards his Lordship, not face the dock, and describe him. The witness states that he has chubby cheeks, narrow eyes, bushy eyebrows but can't tell the colour of his hair because he is wearing a wig.

Court Martial. Charge: Insubordination to a superior officer, in that he at Knightsbridge (i.e. in the Western Desert) when addressed by Company Sergeant Major W. replied 'If bull were music you'd be a f——— brass band.'

Johann Ferdinand Beer came to England as a refugee between the wars. He became an English solicitor, and an erudite and fearless one, but to the end of his days spoke English with a pronounced – and memorable – German accent. He spoke so by choice: soon after his arrival in England, he said, he had a consultation with an Accent Expert. 'I can give you,' said the Expert, 'an English accent for use in Canada, or a Canadian accent for use in England. But an English accent for use in England? That is out of the question.'

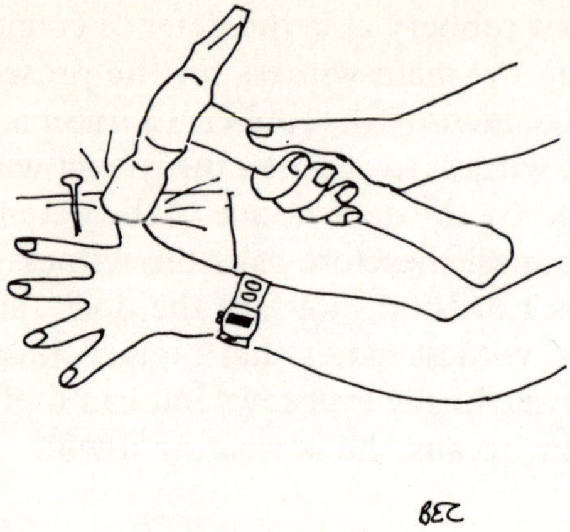

*Damnum Sine Injuria*

*Aggravated arson*

A middle-aged taxi proprietor client of mine died. Some two years before he and his wife had separated and, with no bitterness or disagreement, divorced. As is sometimes the case they appeared to get on better together after divorce than when married. They had two grown up daughters, both of whom had married. The wife, although she had left the matrimonial home, continued to help the husband in his taxi business, returning to the house every day, managing the books with efficiency, answering the telephone etc.

Six months ago Little Miss Piggy came upon the scene and introduced the taxi proprietor to a life style for which he was not suited at his age and from which I believe he ultimately died. Three days before he died he said, unprompted, to his ex-wife, 'Do not worry about your future, I have not changed the will which I made two years ago in your favour. She thinks that I have made a new will because I have told her so under pressure but it is not true.'

The day after the death the ex-wife came to see me in my office. We opened the envelope containing the deceased's will which indeed had been made two years ago in her favour. So far so good. I reassured the ex-wife that her former husband didn't appear to have made a later will. Half an hour later Miss Piggy telephones and introduces herself. She is disappointed to learn there is no later will in my possession in her favour. She states she doesn't intend to let the matter rest. I get on with other business. Later in the day a well-respected firm of London solicitors ring the office. They act for Miss Piggy, they have been advised

...t there is a later will in her favour and have ... believe it will be found in a home safe ... the house by the deceased at Miss Piggy's ...quest. They have the combination and unless we agree to their attending at the house to open the safe and see whether it does indeed contain a will in their client's favour they will take High Court proceedings out for an order that they be allowed access for this purpose. We agreed. It appears we have nothing to lose. An appointment is made but cancelled by Miss Piggy's solicitors when they discovered that, although they believe they know the combination, they do not know which way to turn the knob e.g. left right left right left right etc. The ex-wife becomes tense and upset and when the matter cannot be resolved that evening, insists that it is resolved the following day.

The next day Little Miss Piggy's solicitor ascertains how to open the safe. He gets the information from the person who installed it; curiously, he lives next door to Little Miss Piggy who herself never moved into the deceased's house because the ex-wife was coming in every day. An appointment is made for Thursday morning for the grand opening ceremony. The solicitor for Miss Piggy arrives and in fact I salute his courage. He must know he is putting his head into the lion's den. He represents Her and everybody hates Her. My client, the ex-wife, is there, her daughter and son-in-law are there, they all hate Her, the atmosphere is somewhat tense.

The safe proves to be in the kitchen, in fact it is in the larder. The floor has been built up by about a foot of solid concrete and the safe let into it. The solicitor has the combination which is one of two sets of figures.

*Intention*

*Recklessness*

*Negligence*

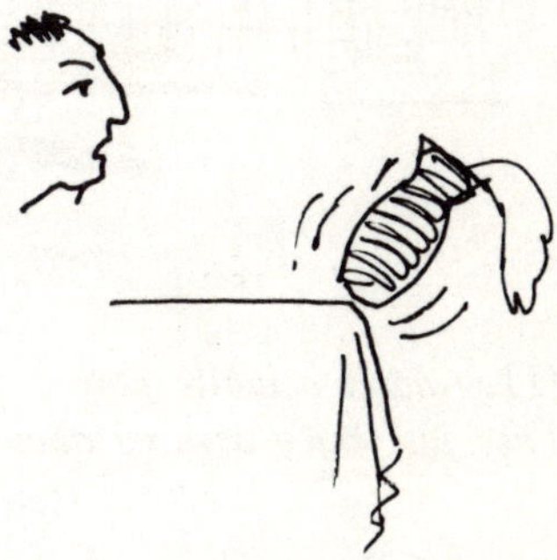

*Strict liability*

*'They don't actually play . . .
They just enjoy arguing about the
score . . .'*

The combination was set by the deceased after the installation of the safe, as was his right to do. The combination was either his birth date in 1922 or his marriage date to the ex-wife in 1944. It turns out it is the date of his marriage, 23 December 1944. The ex-wife nearly has hysterics. She cannot believe that her former husband would be so cruel as to put the date of her marriage on the combination of a safe which may ultimately contain a will in favour of Little Miss Piggy.

The solicitor has to go down on his knees in an attitude of prayer in order to turn the combination knob. He is aware that a steady hand is needed. The light isn't terribly good and he needs to borrow a pair of glasses from the ex-wife in order to see better. He tries several times but cannot get the safe to open. I try several times, I cannot get the safe to open. We all try several times, none of us can get the damn thing to open. The atmosphere becomes electric and the tension unbearable. I leave to return to my office because I have other matters to attend to. Little Miss Piggy's solicitor (who is not having a good week because his office has just burnt down by accident, although he feels the Law Society may not believe him as the auditors were in at the time) decides to call in the safe installer in order to open the safe. The installer arrives only to find that in fact in our various frustrated efforts we had actually opened the safe but failed to pull evenly upon the handle in order to withdraw the safe which is a cylinder set in a tube in the concrete floor. The safe is opened. It is empty. I am advised of the situation by my clients later in the day. I telephone Little Miss Piggy's solicitor and ask of him two things:

(a) that he should charge his client a sum appropriate to the work which he has been required to do; he assures me he will. (b) I ask him what Little Miss Piggy had been told which made her so sure there was another will in her favour in the safe. He sighs: 'She said he told her that everything that he was leaving to her was in the safe'.

It later transpires that Little Miss Piggy had during the course of her short acquaintanceship with the deceased persuaded him to consider selling the taxi business and his house and to buy a bungalow for them to live in. She explained however that since she was in banking in London she had some knowledge of the law and that it would be difficult to purchase the new property in joint names and far better to buy it in her name. Happily the transactions had not taken place at the date of his death.

*A London Magistrates Court, Spring 1986. The witness was about to be sworn.*

Usher: 'What is your religion?'
Witness: 'Eh?'
Bench: 'Are you a Christian?'
Witness: 'John Anthony . . .'
Bench: 'No, no. Do you *believe in God*? Have you *got a religion*?'
Witness: 'Oh no, I haven't got one of those. I'm just an ordinary bloke.'
The witness was allowed to affirm.

*A Conflict Between the Principles of Law and Equity*

Not all courts follow the letter of the Procedural Rules. In a local court applications for occasional licences were being held:
Clerk to the Court: 'Application for an occasional licence on the occasion of the annual gala of the . . . . . . Society.'
Police Inspector: 'Who appears to make this application?'
Chairman of Bench (standing): 'I do.'
Police Inspector: 'No objection Sir.'
Chairman of Bench (now seated): 'This application will be granted.'

The witness was Italian, and excitable. In cross-examination she was accused by counsel of acting in a way which prejudged the case. 'Oh no,' she exclaimed, waving her hands in the direction of the Bench, 'the good Lord will decide the case.'

A tramp is charged with stealing and eating turnips from a roadside field. Such offences being excessively prevalent in the neighbourhood (Norfolk), the magistrates sentenced him to two months imprisonment. On arrival in prison the tramp asks the first prisoner he meets how long he is serving. 'Five years – for rape,' was the reply. 'Good heavens,' replies the tramp, 'you must have eaten the whole bloody field.'

My client was a delightful middle-aged gentleman. Small, impeccably tailored, educated voice. The only unlikely thing about him was his name and that was long and European. Born and brought up in England, he had been something in the City until things had gone badly wrong for him and he'd been made bankrupt; and now he was in the silliest of scrapes. He had been charged with obtaining credit without declaring his bankruptcy: the creditor was his wine merchant and the amount in question was only the price of a case of Medoc, but some busybody had noticed it and had had the lack of judgement to set the inexorable wheels of the law in motion. Sillier even than this, the case was due to be heard at the Old Bailey: that august court still deals with what would in the old days have been little Quarter Sessions cases which arise in the City of London, and this was such a case.

He had no defence. Absent-mindedness was no excuse, and the sole task of his lawyers was to apologise as elegantly as possible. The worst penalty that he could expect was a Conditional Discharge and the client was so advised.

On the appointed day we all turned up at the Bailey and hung around waiting for a court to become available for what was going to be a fifteen-minute plea of guilty. When the public address system called us we were all rather surprised to find that we were directed to the court of a senior, famous and decidedly supercilious Old Bailey judge, a grand gentleman kind of judge, one of the few remaining Olympian-Heights-type judges left over from a more spacious age. The client took his place in the dock, and strange it looked to see this neat little city gentleman sitting affably in the seat normally reserved for those accused of murder, rape and robbery.

'Be upstanding in court,' bellowed the usher and we all rose as the judge sailed majestically in from the wings and took his seat, wrinkling his aristocratic nose.

The charge was read over, the client confessed that he was guilty and prosecuting counsel rose to explain the facts. Two or three sentences into his explanation the judge suddenly stood up. We all scrambled to our feet. 'I can't take this case', he said, and sailed towards his exit right, the usher falling over himself to reach the door before his Lordship did. This kind of thing doesn't happen and we all looked at each other in puzzlement.

Glancing at the dock, however, I noticed that an amused smile was playing around my client's lips. I made may way to the back of the court and leaned up to talk to him.

'Have you any idea what happened?' I asked him.

'Oh, yes,' he said, his eyes twinkling.

'Are you going to tell me?'

'I don't see why not,' he said. 'He was my fag at Eton.'

Young Policeman: '. . . and when I searched the accused she was in possession of forged bank notes.'

Judge: 'Counterfeit?'

Young Policeman: 'Yes, m'Lud, she had two.'

After many years of happy married life between Mr and Mrs X there were constant quarrels resulting in physical violence.

On one occasion when Mr X was worse off for drink he used obscene language and punched Mrs X in the stomach.

To restrain him Mrs X aimed a blow with a kitchen knife and inflicted a wound which led to the removal of the first joint of Mr X's right index-finger.

At her trial for unlawful and malicious wounding, the justices held that the circumstances of the case did not warrant a plea of self-defence and Mrs X was convicted as charged.

They however agreed that she should be 'bound over to keep the peace and be of good behaviour'.

'I cannot keep the "piece",' said Mrs X.

'Why?' asked the magistrates.

'Because they disposed of it at the hospital,' replied Mrs X.

A solicitor and his secretary visited an elderly couple at their home for the purpose of witnessing the execution of their new wills. Both were edentulous, but one complete denture sat on the mantelpiece among the ornaments. Realising the solicitor had spotted them, the lady explained that she had become irritated by her husband's habit of losing his set by leaving them in unsuitable places and had thrown them out. They, therefore, had just the one set between them or 'to do the house' as she put it.

## *Kermit the Frog*

It is always important that a barrister should have his wits about him, and be aware of what is going on around him during a case. Sometimes he should also know what is going on behind him. This is illustrated by the case in which Kermit the Frog perverted the course of justice.

Prosecuting counsel rose to his feet in the Crown Court at the beginning of a shop-lifting case.

'Members of the jury,' he began, 'in this case the defendant went into Woolworths and there stole a toy which I am informed is called Kevin the Frog.'

'*Kermit* the Frog,' said the circuit judge, whose family loved watching that puppet on television.

'I am much obliged, your Honour,' said counsel. 'Anyway, members of the jury, the defendant went into Woolworths where they sold, this, er, Curtis the Frog, and he picked it up and hid it under his jacket. He left the shop without paying for it, and was then stopped by the store detective. The police arrested him, and subsequently charged him with the theft of this, er, Kenneth Toad thing.'

During his speech a clerk appeared at the back of the court carrying a three-foot high effigy of Kermit the Frog, which was the stolen item. It was placed immediately behind counsel.

The jury fidgeted uneasily, not being sure if they were allowed to laugh. But some temptations are too much even for a circuit judge, who leaned forward in his chair, and addressed counsel.

'I think,' he said, '*your learned junior* has some instructions for you.'

*Oath for administrators with will annexed*

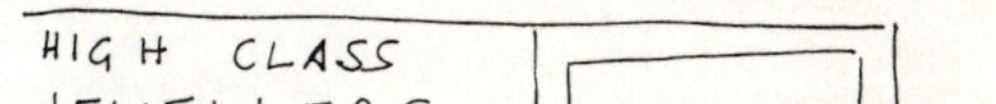


*Reasonable suspicion*

The prosecuting counsel, who had no junior in the case, turned round in some surprise. He came face to face with Kermit the Frog. There was so much laughter that the case came to a halt.

A deaf old man appeared in the dock on a charge of gross indecency. At the end of the trial the judge said to him 'You are a filthy old fellow and you will go to prison for two years.' 'Eh?' said the old man. The warder (they were called warders in those days) then leaned forward and shouted into the old man's ear 'His Lordship says you are a dirty old bugger and you'll go to jail for three years'. 'Warder', said the judge, 'while you may paraphrase my sentiments you have no power to vary the sentence.'

Another exchange between judge and counsel. It starts with the judge reading from a probation report:

Judge: 'The Probation Officer says in his report "I understand that the defendant has a conviction in the magistrates' court." What does that mean?'
Counsel: 'Your Honour, I deplore the use of the expression "I understand", it is ambiguous, ambivalent and decidedly unhelpful.'
Judge: 'That may be so but what is the position?'
Counsel: 'I understand that he was bound over.'

*'I've seen him address the ball for three days . . .'*

That the business of lawyers should be confined to minding their own is a sentiment to which many non-lawyers would claim allegiance and which finds poignant expression in the following text of a letter allegedly sent by Sir Henri Deterding to his manager in New York in 1916. Sir Henri was born a Dutchman in 1866 and died a naturalised Briton in 1939 at least 240,000 acres of oil fields the richer. Among his other claims to fame and/or notoriety were his directorship of Shell and his prominence as a Nazi supporter.

The letter also provides a good illustration of how, even in 1916, attitudes to lawyers on either side of the Atlantic were rather different:

Dear Mr. Luyks,

I duly received yours of the 22nd ult. regarding Messrs. Rice & Lyons' remuneration.

You gave me rather a start with your letter, because I gather from it that you employ solicitors much more often than we would ever dream of doing. Although we have an enormous business here, we very rarely consult lawyers. We only do so when there is really a legal difference or legal difficulty, whilst it seems to me that you employ them practically in every instance.

Lawyers are not business people, however large a lawyer's experience may be, in the conduct of business he is absolutely useless. A lawyer placed at the head of a concern, would soon bring the business to rack and ruin. He is not a creative genius, he is able to give his opinion, if a case is laid before him, but to ask a lawyer to draw up a contract for you is a most foolish thing to do, and this is bound to lead to trouble. Our custom here is to draw up a contract before having seen the lawyer and then to ask him to put it in a more legal shape. Such a contract is more likely to embody the spirit of what has been agreed upon than one drawn up by the lawyer; to ask his opinion as to what you should do or not do is the worst possible way of conducting business, which should be kept as far as possible from the lawyers.

It seems to me from your letter as if the lawyers are a kind of department to your business. Their idea that we should be inclined to give them a fixed fee is absurd, but what astonishes me most is their proposal that you should make an arrangement, by which one member of their firm should give practically his entire time to the conduct of our affairs. We would never think of such an arrangement. We do not wish a lawyer to give his entire time to our business. We have not got daily disputes, neither do we want to create them. A lawyer is absolutely unfit as a business man, he is to give us advice if trouble arises and if you employ him, say six times a year, that can be considered the average maximum. I do not think we employ a lawyer many more times and our total lawyer's bill here is *considerably* less than yours. Messrs. Rice & Lyons' statement that at the present time the daily routinc business of our Company consumes the time and efforts of one member of their firm, is a revelation to me. How can you conduct business in such a way! I hate to see a lawyer in our office, if I want him I go to *his* office and limit the conversation to the shortest possible period. Allowing a lawyer to be practically in daily touch with me, would certainly take 90% of my time which ought to be devoted to money making and not to discussing legal squabbles or legal phraseologies.

Yours sincerely,
(Sgnd.) H. Deterding

13th September, 1916

The following is perhaps an apocryphal tale, although lawyers can be found to vouch for its truth:

Very junior counsel was clearly in a hurry when mitigating for his client, a prostitute, and he confidently informed the judge: 'Your Honour, the best point that can be made is that this still young lady, who has for so long now stooped to the way of life giving rise to this charge, this young lady now has gainful, law-abiding, respectable employment.'

The judge intervened:

'Yes, but what exactly is her newfound employment . . .?'

Junior counsel frantically turned and took very hurried instructions from his solicitor and unthinkingly announced to the expectant court:

'Your Honour, she is a tool hardener in a local engineering factory.'

The court was hurriedly adjourned.

In a case where a defendant was charged with stealing an aqua pot (a type of self-watering plant holder) the judge gave the jury the following helpful guidance:

'Aqua is after the Latin word for water and pot is after the English word for pot.'

*Res Extincta*

## *The Bailey Juror*

The heat in the old courts at the Old Bailey is overpowering, and during the course of an afternoon many a juror has fallen asleep. Nobody makes a fuss of course but the judge tends to notice it when the public in the gallery start to titter, especially if the unfortunate person begins to snore. A useful remedy is to knock a heavy book off counsel's bench to the floor, which usually brings the slumberer around with a jolt.

The tale is told of such an occurrence during a rape trial when the victim was giving her evidence in chief. There, in the back row of the jury box a man, his eyelids too heavy to fight, nodded off. Next to him a pretty young blonde was perturbed but said nothing.

The victim was being asked what it was that the prisoner had said he was going to do to her. She was overcome with embarrassment. She couldn't say the words. Not to the judge. Not in open court.

His Lordship determined that she should write down what the rapist had said and the note was duly passed along the front row of the jury. It reached the back row and passed slowly along. The blonde read the note, nudged her neighbour awake and passed it to him.

He read the note, looked at the blonde, went beetroot red, grinned, screwed up the note and put it in his pocket.

Leeds Magistrates' Court (1983): solicitor when applying for bail to magistrates, 'As murders go, this was not a bad one . . .'

*'. . . and finally m'lord . . .'*

One of the most competent (and tallest) members of the Junior Bar was instructed to act for a plaintiff in the County Court in the 'Black Country'. The plaintiff, a farmer, claimed damages against the manufacturer/supplier of sheep dip, alleging that the dip was defective. Counsel took the plaintiff's expert witness through his proof of evidence without a hitch.

Counsel for the defendant suggested a number of reasons for the failure of the dip. Each time the expert accepted the reason as a possibility, to the great dismay of the plaintiff and *his* counsel.

When counsel for the plaintiff was asked by the judge if there was to be any re-examination, the plaintiff's counsel slowly unwound himself into a standing position, glared at the expert and muttered menacingly 'Goodbye'.

It is too easy for an advocate to assume that he has a witness in a corner from which the witness cannot escape. In a case of driving without due care and attention the advocate was cross-examining an eye-witness to the occurrence.

Advocate: 'You say, Mrs. X, that you saw the car for no apparent reason career across the road, run into the stone wall, demolish the wall, with stones all over the road, and then go through the wall and into the field?'

Lady witness: 'Yes.'

Advocate: 'How do you explain then that there was not a single scratch or mark anywhere on the car?'

Lady witness: (quick as a flash) 'A miracle.'

The first thing my pupil-master taught me was that he never lost a case; though occasionally a judge might 'take an old-fashioned view'.

Counsel was defending at a Midlands court a man accused of assault. The defence was that the accused was provoked by the way he was spoken to by the victim. When the Court adjourned for the luncheon break counsel was just about to address the jury so it was decided to postpone it until 2 pm. At the appointed time everyone was in his place in court except one juror. At a minute past 2 the juror was pushed into the jury box by an usher. The juror looked like a frightened rabbit. Before he could be properly seated, counsel, looking at him, loudly exclaimed: 'You f——— bastard!' All thought this outburst was aimed at the little man cowering on the end of the jury bench, none more so than the juror himself. Counsel paused and continued: 'Those words, members of the jury, were the words uttered by the injured party just before my client lost his temper and struck him'. The jury acquitted without retiring!

There was once a judge with one good eye and one glass eye. It was said of him that it was easy to tell the difference: the one with the gleam of compassion in it was the glass eye.

*Enquiries Before Contract*

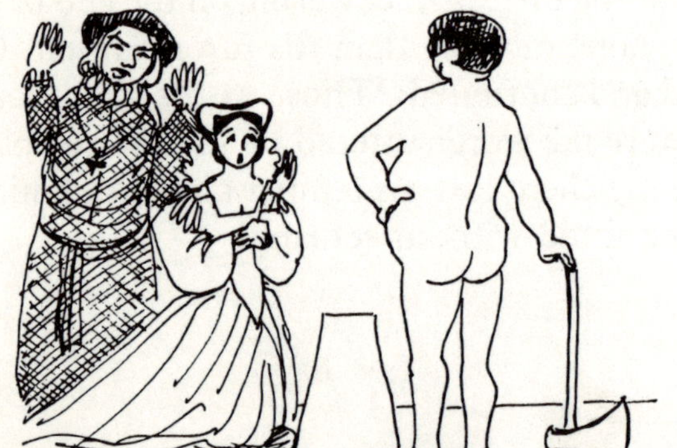

*Improper execution*

Mr Justice Rigby Swift was hearing a trial in which an elderly lady sought to challenge the will of her late sister, whose considerable estate was to pass out of the family. Swift J. inclined to hurry the proceedings, having formed the view that the plaintiff's case was lacking in substance.

'Madam, why are you bringing this case?' he asked the plaintiff during her evidence in chief. She replied that she thought she had every right to do so.

He next enquired if she had been so advised by counsel. 'Yes,' she said. The judge probed further. 'By counsel appearing for you?' When she answered 'No,' Swift J. asked by whom? 'My nephew', replied the lady, explaining that he had recently been called to the bar.

'Madam, did he charge you a fee for his advice?'

'Of course not,' she said. 'He is my nephew.'

'Madam, have you ever been told that advice is worth exactly what you pay for it?'

A young police constable was giving evidence for the first time at the Crown Court at a provincial market town. He described his perambulation through the streets at 3 a.m. on a winter's day.

'I saw the accused looking in a shop window. I said to him "Why are you looking in that shop window at this time of day?". He replied in a language which I now understand to be Urdu and I said to him "I am not satisfied with your explanation and I require you to accompany me to the police station".'

In the Leeds Magistrates Court a case was being dealt with by a member of the Leeds Crown Prosecuting Solicitors Department. The man was a clown. All the way through the case he was persistently objecting to questions, asking objectionable questions and asking for adjournments so that he could check on the law to see whether he could raise another objection to something else. The case dragged its wearisome way through until the point where the prosecuting solicitor was cross examining Bill Kerr, a psychiatrist from Clifton Hospital, York who had prepared a report on the defendant. The cross examination went as follows:

'Did you examine this lady at all, Dr. Kerr?'

'Yes I carried out a clinical examination.'

'Does that mean you just talked to her?'

'No, it means I carried out a clinical examination.'

'But you didn't have to examine her in any way did you?'

'Well, I may have taken her pulse but nothing more.'

'So that apart from that you just talked to her?'

'I am a psychiatrist and that is how a psychiatrist carries out a clinical examination.'

'Well, what do you mean by a clinical examination?'

'Look, it takes seven years to train a psychiatrist, how do you expect me to answer that question in two minutes?'

At this point the Chairman of the Bench lent forward and with a sigh said 'I quite agree Dr. Kerr. I am *told* it takes a long time to train a lawyer too.'

New jury panels are called on a Monday with jurors being required either for a fortnight or three weeks. They come from a wide area surrounding any particular Crown Court centre.

The Crown Court at Wood Green opened at about the same time as a nearby shopping precinct development called Wood Green Shopping City.

It was ten minutes past two on a Monday afternoon at Wood Green Crown Court. A trial had started that morning and the jury, all members of a new panel, had been told to be back from lunch for two o'clock. The judge, if impatient, did not show it: he caused enquiries to be made about a missing juror who had failed to return.

At half past two the lady in question came into court, took her place meekly in the jury box, since everybody was waiting, and placed a large D.H. Evans carrier bag by her feet.

'Good afternoon, madam,' said the judge. She nodded back, a little embarrassed.

'And may I ask where you have been this lunch time?' he continued.

'Well, I don't live very near here, and so don't come to this shopping centre very often. I went into D.H. Evans.'

'And, madam, may I enquire as to whether you purchased anything?'

'Yes, actually I bought a dress.'

'How nice! Would you like to show it to us.'

The woman picked up the bag and, self-consciously at first, though not for long, took out her new dress and showed it to the court.

'That is very nice madam,' the judge said

approvingly, 'you have very good taste.'

'Thank you, your Honour.'

'I wonder, would you mind telling us how much it cost?'

'Well normally I wouldn't dream of spending this much on a dress, but it is nice, and . . . well, it cost £50.'

The judge stopped smiling and said firmly, 'Yes, madam, and that is the amount that you will be fined for keeping this court waiting.'

The judge's large bundle of papers lay unopened on his bench but the name of the plaintiff, a large Japanese corporation, was plain to see. Showing some of that fairness for which our judiciary is famed, he said to counsel:

'Gentlemen, before this case commences, I think you both should know that during the war I spent three years as an unwilling guest of the Japanese army in Burma. If, therefore, either of you feels I should not try this case then I will listen sympathetically to your application.'

Counsel conferred and both agreed that their faith in our judiciary made such an application unnecessary.

'Very well,' said the judge, 'I find for the defendant, with costs.'

*Res Ispa Loquitur*

A policeman was giving evidence in Leeds Magistrates court against the defendant who was accused of using a car with defective brakes. It was the first time that he had ever appeared in court and therefore he went over his evidence very carefully to make sure that he knew it exactly. When he was called to give evidence he was sworn and after stating his name and rank he was invited to say what his evidence was. He took a deep breath and then in one breath he said 'On the 15th February 1979 I was on duty in The Headrow Leeds when I had reason to suspect that the vehicle registration number 452 VWX was being driven with brakes which were not in proper working order. I therefore called the vehicle to stop asked the driver to get out and found that I and my co-driver were able to push the vehicle against the hand brake for a distance of twenty-five yards without meeting any resistance whatsoever.'

He then paused for breath and at that stage the Chairman said helpfully, 'On the level, officer?'. The officer replied swiftly, 'Oh, without a word of a lie, your Worship.'

Supposedly overheard in the Athenaeum:

1st Judge: 'Can't think what the world's coming to, all these young fellows nowadays seem to sleep around with any old floozie they can lay their hands on. I know I never slept with my wife before I was married – how about you?'

2nd Judge: 'Really couldn't say old chap, what was her maiden name?'

Shortly after I qualified, an exceedingly beautiful young lady with eyes of saxon blue arrived in my office demanding a divorce on the grounds of non-consummation.

Putting to one side my utter disbelief, I asked how long she had been married. 'One week,' was her answer. It transpired that her husband was a gypsy and had been drunk at all material times.

I ventured that she should perhaps wait upon events a little longer, especially as in those days one could not petition for divorce during the first three years of a marriage without leave of the court.

Undoubtedly she found the laws delays irksome, and I was obliged to explain that leave could be obtained in cases of extreme hardship or depravity – though there appeared to have been a singular lack of depravity, and the hardship of which she was complaining was not one recognized by the courts.

In desperation, I counselled that if she were to provide her husband with evidence of adultery at so early a stage in the marriage, he might be provoked into petitioning and the court could well grant him leave.

'This adultery,' she enquired, fixing me with her blue eyes, 'Can I get it on Legal Aid?'

A defendant in the Crown Court had been found guilty of an offence against the criminal law. When the judge was passing sentence the defendant was heard to say 'Beam me up Scotty' as he looked upwards.

In 1944 whilst an officer serving in Italy, I was asked to defend a fellow officer in a court-martial on a charge of drunkenness. I was not at that time a qualified solicitor but had passed the then Solicitors Intermediate examination, not without difficulty, in 1939.

My client had been found lying in a ditch near an American camp and it was alleged that his breath smelt heavily of alcohol. Our defence was that he had just arrived from England, had lost his way in the dark and been knocked unconscious by an American sergeant.

A very distinguished looking Judge-Advocate appeared at the court-martial and his duty was to sum up the evidence to the members of the court, which he did in a way which was very agreeable to me, short, to the point and dead in my favour. I remember his saying 'Drunkenness is like an elephant, easy to see but difficult to define.' The court retired for about three minutes and duly brought in a verdict of 'not guilty'.

My client, the former prisoner, his best friend and myself were much elated and went next door to the Officers' Club where we celebrated well but none too wisely. We eventually staggered unsteadily into the Neapolitan sunshine and there on the other side of the street was the chief prosecution witness, the Provost-Marshall and the Judge-Advocate. We dived into a shop in the Galleria Umberto lest we were seen as I knew there was no chance of defeating a similar charge if it had been brought against us.

Over the past years I have often wondered what would have happened to my career, both military and legal, if that Judge-Advocate had seen me, because his name was Elwyn-Jones who became Lord Chancellor!

A barrister was mitigating for a youth convicted of assault:

'I invite your Honour to view this assault as not so much a planned attack but more of an over-reaction on the defendant's part. He was sitting in a public house when he was urgently informed by a friend that his brother was being battered in the local fish and chip shop!'

A foreign gentleman became increasingly irate at counsel's vigorous cross examination and attempts to discredit him by – amongst other things – being dismissive of his understanding of English. The defendant could contain himself no longer and said 'You think I know damned nothing but I can assure you I know damned all'.

The judge passing sentence on a criminal in a tricky case concluded 'In summary I do not know whether you are guilty or not. There is an element of doubt in this case, but you are not getting the benefit of it. I am sending you to prison for six months. If you are guilty you have got off lightly. If you are innocent let it be a lesson to you.'

The following legal definition of the word 'and' is believed to be of transatlantic origin:

*and* [Short Form]

'and' shall mean 'and' unless the context shall otherwise require but subject nevertheless to the provisions of paragraph (0) of Section 35 of the definition of the term 'but for', and shall not mean or include but, for, butfor, or, although, whereas, now therefore, grant, convey, assign, cede, transfer, warrant, hypothecate, mortgage, pledge, charge, building, Albania, plant, factory, mill, structure, pipe, improvement, street, way, alley, passage, sewer, right, railroad track, dock, water, water course, easement, estate, right, franchise, interest, privilege, liberties, servitude, hereditament, appurtenance, erection, fixture, rent, revenue, issue, earning, income, products, profit, estate, title, interest, property, claim, demand, reversion, alteration, modification, amendment, change, extension, renewal, void, voidable, lease, contract, agreement, real, personal, movable, immovable, bond, note, debt, indebtedness, secured, unsecured, Chateau de Rougement, Great Western Sugar Producers or *pari passu*, all of which terms are hereinbefore or hereinafter defined; *provided, however*, that if the word 'and' shall appear in the plural, it shall mean, unless the context otherwise requires but subject nevertheless to the provisions of subpart (D) of clause (O) of subparagraph (Y) of paragraph (L) of subsection (E) of Section 4 of the definition of the word 'may', that there is a typographical error and such word shall be deemed to be null, void and without effect unless otherwise agreed to by the parties hereto or their permitted successors or assigns in writing; and *further provided*, that notwithstanding any of the foregoing or anything else herein contained to the contrary, if a dispute should arise among the parties hereto or their successors or assigns as to the meaning or interpretation of the word 'and', such dispute shall be submitted for binding arbitration to a single arbitrator, selected by Counsel for the Bondholders, which arbitrator shall be any past, present or future Mayor of Matinecock, Long Island, without regard to any possible or probable conflict of interest on the part of such arbitrator, and any determination by such arbitrator shall be final and binding on all parties hereto and their successors and assigns notwithstanding that such determination may be arbitrary, capricious, unfair, inequitable, inconsistent with any prior determination by such arbitrator, or incomprehensible to a reasonable man, a prudent man, a reasonably prudent man or any man, and any attempt to appeal or object to such determination will constitute an Event of Default (as hereinafter defined) hereunder.

This is attributed to His Honour Judge Kirkhouse Jenkins who died some years ago. A solicitor appeared in court wearing a suit and gown and bands but with a fancy waistcoat. When he rose to his feet the judge said 'Mr Smith I cannot hear you.' The advocate, thinking that the judge was slightly deaf, raised his voice whereupon His Honour said 'Mr Smith, it is not your voice I cannot hear – I cannot hear you because your waistcoat is too loud.'

In my capacity as Deputy Coroner I had occasion to deal with the death of an ex-coal miner aged ninety-eight. Pneumoconiosis was a contributory factor. Normally in such cases one would arrange for a postmortem to be carried out, and an inquest to be opened and a verdict of death due to industrial disease returned at the inquest. However, in view of his age, I considered that this procedure might be dispensed with and the matter reported to Registrar of Births and Deaths, and dealt with by way of a Coroner's Part A certificate. I did, however, think that I first ought to check as to whether or not he had left a widow; if so, the National Coal Board would require a postmortem to be carried out before paying any compensation on pension which might be due to the pneumoconiosis. I therefore telephoned the house of the deceased and the telephone was answered by his son who was aged sixty-two. I explained to him the reason for my telephone call and asked him 'Is your mother still alive?' He replied 'I do not know, I will go to the kitchen and ask her.'

My mother-in-law's solicitor was reputed to be the most hated man in Liverpool. A client once visited him and was given unpalatable advice.

The client leant down and took a revolver from his briefcase, shot at the solicitor and ran out into the street. The solicitor's managing clerk ran after the client shouting 'Come back! come back! you fool, you missed.'

*'. . . Could you lend me a fiver to Friday? . . .'*

A witness in a drunk-in-charge case, describing the defendant, turned to the judge and said 'He was as drunk as a judge your honour.' The judge looked down and said 'Surely you mean as drunk as a lord.' The witness replied 'Yes my Lord.'

Scene: Derby County Court
Time: Early 1960s
Judge: Sir Henry Braund
Court: Judgment
The judgment debtor arrives in the box to disclose that one side of his prominent moustache had been shaved off. Sir Henry took this as an act of ridicule of him and the court and let the debtor know his feelings. Turning to the means questionnaire completed by the debtor, he discovered that he appeared to be very lowly paid for an occupation shown as 'glass engineer'. When interrogated by the judge he revealed, amidst laughter from the well of the court, that he was a window cleaner. Needless to say: pay in seven days or 42 days jail.

Sir Raymond Everthed Charter of the Rolls, when practising at the Bar in Birmingham, is said to have made the classic comment:

'This case is so one sided I am surprised to find the evidence is printed on both sides of the paper.'

*Trade Fixtures*

*Uncertainty of Object*

A man called to see a rather newly qualified solicitor and explained that he had been charged with obtaining a cheque by false pretences. He said that he thought that the best way to deal with the matter was to plead not guilty in the magistrates court, listen to the prosecution case, submit that there was no case to answer, and if that was turned down elect to go for trial at Quarter Sessions. The solicitor asked him if he had been in trouble before and was told that he had 'a bit of form'.

The solicitor was not entirely without experience and said that he would like to get the question of costs sorted out straightaway. The defendant said there was no prospect of his getting legal aid and so the solicitor said he wanted some money in advance. Unfortunately he then showed his inexperience by asking for £30.

'Right, squire,' said the defendant who walked out.

The solicitor wondered if he would see him again but a few days later the sum of £30 arrived as promised. About two days before the hearing the solicitor heard that the case was going to have to be adjourned because a witness was ill, and tried to get in touch with the defendant at his place of work. When the phone was answered the following conversation took place.

'Could I speak to Mr. Smith please?'

'You'll not find him here.'

'I am sorry, he told me that he worked there.'

'Aye he did, but he pinched £30 off me.'

His Honour Judge Crowther sentencing a 'welshing' bookie: 'You must service 69 days in prison – on my calculation with remission for good conduct you should be free just in time for the flat.'

Solicitors in property transactions frequently use printed forms, for general enquiries as to the property being purchased, deletions to be made and specific questions to be added to suit the particular transaction. A young solicitor acting on the purchase of property in the West End of London, omitted to make any deletions and enquired 'Is the owner of the property responsible for the upkeep of any sea wall or dyke?' Needless to say the reply came back 'Please indicate what sea washes the shores of Piccadilly, London.'

*A Will of a City financier:*

To my wife I leave her lover and the knowledge that I wasn't the fool she thought I was.

To my son I leave the pleasure of earning a living. For thirty five years he thought the pleasure was mine. He was mistaken.

To my daughter I leave £150,000. She will need it. The only good business her husband ever did was to marry her.

To my valet I leave all my clothes he has been steadily stealing from me for the past ten years.

To my chauffeur I leave all my cars. He almost ruined them and I want him to have the satisfaction of finishing the job.

To my partner I leave the suggestion that he takes some other man in with him if he expects to do any business.

And lastly to my cousin Louis who always wanted be remembered in my Will – hello Louis.

The Rules Committee of the European Parliament works very closely with the Legal Affairs Committee; it is largely composed of lawyers, and at the beginning had to rewrite all the rules for the new Parliament. We held an immense number of meetings for many hours at a time, amending all the rules orally with the interpreters in the interpretation booths around us, behind glass, doing their best to keep up with what was going on. For weeks arguments ensued on every single word in such expressions (in eight languages) as 'that the question now put do be adjourned etc. etc.,' all in the jargon of the national parliaments, each country having totally different ideas as to procedure and as to the jargon to describe that procedure. We worked our way through all the rules, amending as we went along in our eight languages but all orally. Then the result was taken to the Plenary Session of the Parliament where we had to have a two-thirds majority in favour of our hundreds of amendments. A full house had gathered for the great occasion. It was then discovered that the numbering of the rules in the different languages was different and that all our deep discussions over the previous weeks in the Rules Committee must have taken place with each member looking at the original text in his own language and debating it heatedly against members from other nationalities who were, in fact, debating completely different rules equally heatedly. None of us had ever noticed this during our long meetings and, furthermore, we thought we had ended up with an agreed set of rules. The matter was so embarrassing to us lawyers in the Parliament that we had to withdraw all our proposals and start from scratch.

*'. . . The pressure's beginning to tell – poor chap never gets to sleep before lunch . . .'*

A barrister, making a plea in mitigation on behalf of two defendants in the Norwich Crown Court, began: 'Smith is a young man with a very low IQ, is a schizophrenic depressive and unemployed. Jones is less gifted.'

During the course of a simple trial in the Norwich Crown Court counsel passed each other notes as discreetly as possible. This obviously did not go unnoticed, because after the jury had retired to consider the verdict they indicated to the judge that they had a question, and they returned to the court-room. The foreman then said that the jury wanted to know the details of the notes that were being passed between counsel, as they thought they might be relevant to their deliberations. The judge asked the senior counsel to pass up the notes, which he duly did, and the judge, without any sign of emotion whatsoever, read the notes. He then looked up and said 'Members of the Jury, it would appear that Counsel for the Prosecution and Counsel for the Defence have been concentrating their efforts more on wagering bets about the likely Test Match score than on the merits of this case.'

The definition of 'barrister' in the dictionary is between 'bankrupt' and 'bastard'.

*'I'm sorry, sir, you can't go in there with those hands.'*

It was in the early 1930's and the client had died. He was a mining engineer, specialising in West Africa. He was married and yet had left a Will leaving the whole of his estate to another woman, whom he appointed Executor. The solicitors prepared the probate papers and, not knowing the status of the lady concerned, left a blank in the two affidavits. They sent the probate papers to her in Africa, for swearing, and in their covering letter requested her to insert her occupation/status before swearing the affidavits. Back came the papers in due course, duly completed and her occupation/status was given as 'Gold digger – Spinster'.

Some time ago I acted for a man who had lost a finger at work. The claim was successfully dealt with. Some eighteen months later I received a letter from him saying that he had been at work when a grindstone exploded; due to inadequate guarding, a large piece of the grindstone caught him very painfully in the groin area. From his hospital bed he wrote to ask me if I would act for him again, telling me that when he had regained consciousness after an emergency operation the surgeon had informed him that he had regrettably had to remove his right 'tentacle'.

I was left with the view that it was a very unfortunate incident but that if he had been left with another seven tentacles after the injury, the claim would not be worth a great deal. Needless to say, after further investigation it was found to be a spelling mistake!

Two cases concerning Mr Justice Vaisey.

The first was a case involving a patent for shoe boxes for the women's arm of the Royal Navy. Some days after the case had begun and his desk was covered with these boxes (which were inventive in that they nested inside each other), and there had been much discussion of the boxes and the WRENS and the shoes, Mr Justice Vaisey suddenly asked, picking up one of the boxes: 'Is this where the bird flies in?'

The second case concerning him (and he was a teetotaller) dealt with whisky emphatically not made in Scotland, in triangular bottles with labels with new moons printed on them, which in a smoke-filled, ill-lit bar in South America, looked like the shadows in the dimples of the genuine Dimple Whisky bottle. The point was to show that valuable goodwill depended on the shape of the bottle. After a lot of argument Mr Justice Vaisey said: 'You mean it's like the embossed lines on a Roses lime juice bottle?' We knew we had lost immediately, as it was clear that the judge never ventured further than Roses lime juice.

Leeds Magistrates' Court:

Defence solicitor – 'My client came through the door in his pyjamas.'
Prosecuting solicitor – 'I didn't notice there was a door in his pyjamas.'

A prisoner in the dock was asked by the judge if had anything to say, and replied 'F—— all'. The judge, who hadn't heard, asked the clerk what the prisoner had said. The clerk dutifully replied 'F—— all, my Lord'. 'That's funny,' said the judge, 'I am sure I saw his lips move.'

In the days before partition it was a criminal offence in Ireland to ferment alcohol. Once it was proved that the defendant was in possession of a 'still', the burden of proof was on the defendant to prove he didn't use it. The Irish defendant was found in possession of a 'still' and had the above explained to him by the court but he couldn't for the life of him understand it. As much as the judge tried to explain that the Irishman did have the equipment, the defendant repeated that he didn't ferment alcohol with it. After many outbursts from the defendant the judge finally said to the defendant 'Are there any other offences you would like me to take into consideration?' 'Yes your Honour,' replied the defendant, 'Rape – I have the equipment.'

Magistrate to defendant (Leeds Magistrates' Court):
'You will be fined £15 – how can you pay?'

Defendant: '£5 per week.'

Magistrate: 'That's not good enough – you will pay the whole fine in 28 days.'

*'. . . and ten happy Christmases to you too, sir . . .'*

In the days when the easiest way to minimise estate duty was to give it to one's family and survive five years a certain client had survived four years and six months when at summer tea in the garden with his family he collapsed. He was obviously dead but the eldest son was concerned about the legal arrangements. After consultation the deceased was placed in the deep freeze. At Christmas when the five years had expired he was disinterred and thawed out. The doctor was called and confirmed death but explained that the coroner would have to be informed as he, the doctor, could not give a certificate. Later he contacted the family to confirm that the coroner had issued a certificate and the death was natural, but he had a query. Although it was said that the deceased had died whilst eating Christmas dinner with his family it was clear that he had just enjoyed a large helping of strawberries and cream. Quickly the eldest son explained 'That is easily understood doctor – you see we have a deep freeze.'

*You Cannabiserious*

A barrister was mitigating for a drug user and pusher when he accidentally exemplified the fact that many a true word is spoken in jest:

'It is admitted, Your Honour, that this young man has committed serious offences but in my submission it is quite clear from the probation report herein that he still has a good deal to offer society.'

*Equity leans against Double Portions*

*Trespass and Rape?*

The case of R v. Collins was heard by the Appeal Court in 1972. The court's judgment was delivered by Lord Justice Edmund Davies.

This is about as extraordinary a case as my brethren and I have ever heard either on the Bench or while at the Bar. Stephen William George Collins was convicted on 29th October 1971 at Essex Assizes of burglary with intent to commit rape and he was sentenced to 21 months' imprisonment. He is a nineteen-year-old youth, and he appeals against that conviction by the certificate of the trial judge. The terms in which that certificate is expressed reveals that the judge was clearly troubled about the case and the conviction.

Let me relate the facts. Were they put into a novel or portrayed on the stage, they would be regarded as being so improbable as to be unworthy of serious consideration and as verging at times on farce. At about two o'clock in the early morning of Saturday, 24th July 1971, a young lady of eighteen went to bed at her mother's home in Colchester. She had spent the evening with her boyfriend. She had taken a certain amount of drink, and it may be that this fact affords some explanation of her inability to answer satisfactorily certain crucial questions put to her. She has the habit of sleeping without wearing night apparel in a bed which is very near the lattice-type window of her room. At one stage on her evidence she seemed to be saying that the bed was close up against the window which, in accordance with her practice, was wide open. In the photographs which we have before us, however, there appears to be a gap of some sort between the two, but the bed was clearly quite near the window. At about 3.30 or 4.00 a.m. she awoke and she then saw in the moonlight a vague form crouched in the open window. She was unable to remember, and this is important, whether the form was on the outside of the window sill or on that part of the sill which was inside the room, and for reasons which will later become clear, that seemingly narrow point is of crucial importance. The young lady then realised several things: first of all that the form in the window was that of a male; secondly that he was a naked male; and thirdly that he was a naked male with an erect penis. She also saw in the moonlight that his hair was blond. She thereupon leapt to the conclusion that her boy-friend, with whom for some time she had been on terms of regular and frequent sexual intimacy, was paying her an ardent nocturnal visit. She promptly sat up in bed, and the man descended from the sill and joined her in bed and they had full sexual intercourse. But there was something about him which made her think that things were not as they usually were between her and her boyfriend. The length of his hair, his voice as they had exchanged what was described as 'love talk', and other features led her to the conclusion that somehow there was something different. So she turned on the bed-side light, saw that her companion was not her boyfriend and slapped the face of the intruder, who was none other than the appellant. He said to her, 'Give me a good time tonight', and got hold of her arm, but she bit him and told him to go. She then went into the bathroom and he promptly vanished.

The complainant said that she would not have

agreed to intercourse if she had known that the person entering her room was not her boyfriend. But there was no suggestion of any force having been used on her, and the intercourse which took place was undoubtedly effected with no resistance on her part.

The appellant was seen by the police at about 10.30 a.m. later that same morning. According to the police, the conversation which took place then elicited these points: He was very lustful the previous night. He had taken a lot of drink, and we may here note that drink (which to him is a very real problem) had brought this young man into trouble several times before, but never for an offence of this kind. He went on to say that he knew the complainant because he had worked around her house. On this occasion, desiring sexual intercourse – and according to the police evidence he had added that he was determined to have a girl, by force if necessary, although that part of the police evidence he challenged – he went on to say that he walked around the house, saw a light in an upstairs bedroom, and he knew that this was the girl's bedroom. He found a step ladder, leaned it against the wall and climbed up and looked into the bedroom. What he could see inside through the wide open window was a girl who was naked and asleep. So he descended the ladder and stripped off all his clothes, with the exception of his socks, because apparently he took the view that if the girl's mother entered the bedroom it would be easier to effect a rapid escape if he had his socks on than if he was in his bare feet. That is a matter about which we are not called on to express any view, and would in any event find ourselves unable to express one. Having undressed, he then climbed the ladder and pulled himself up on to the window sill. His version of the matter is that he was pulling himself in when she awoke. She then got up and knelt on the bed, she put her arms around his neck and body, and she seemed to pull him into the bed. He went on:

> '. . . I was rather dazed, because I didn't think she would want to know me. We kissed and cuddled for about ten or fifteen minutes and then I had it away with her but found it hard because I had had so much to drink.'

The police officer said to the appellant:

> 'It appears that it was your intention to have intercourse with this girl by force if necessary and it was only pure coincidence that this girl was under the impression that you were her boyfriend and apparently that is why she consented to allowing you to have sexual intercourse with her.'

It was alleged that he then said:

> 'Yes, I feel awful about this. It is the worst day of my life, but I know it could have been worse.'

Thereupon the officer said to him – and the appellant challenges this – 'What do you mean, you know it could have been worse?' to which he is alleged to have replied:

> 'Well, my trouble is drink and I got very frustrated. As I've told you I only wanted to have it away with a girl and I'm only glad I haven't really hurt her.'

Then he made a statement under caution, in the course of which he said:

*A property adjustment order*

*Affidavit of Plight and Condition*

> 'When I stripped off and got up the ladder I made up my mind that I was going to try and have it away with this girl. I feel terrible about this now, but I had too much to drink. I am sorry for what I have done.'

In the course of his testimony, the appellant said that he would not have gone into the room if the girl had not knelt on the bed and beckoned him into the room. He said that if she had objected immediately to his being there or to his having intercourse he would not have persisted. While he was keen on having sexual intercourse that night, it was only if he could find someone who was willing. He strongly denied having told the police that he would, if necessary, have pushed over some girl for the purpose of having intercourse.

There was a submission of no case to answer on the ground that the evidence did not support the charge, particularly that ingredient of it which had reference to entry into the house 'as a trespasser'. But the submission was overruled, and as we have already related, he gave evidence.

Now, one feature of the case which remained at the conclusion of the evidence in great obscurity is where exactly the appellant was at the moment when, according to him, the girl manifested that she was welcoming him. Was he kneeling on the sill outside the window or was he already inside the room, having climbed through the window frame, and kneeling on the inner sill? . . . thereby having committed the trespass prior to her welcoming invitation.

Unless the jury were entirely satisfied that the appellant made an effective and substantial entry into the bedroom without the complainant doing or saying anything to cause him to believe that she was consenting to his entering it, he ought not to be convicted of the offence charged. The point is a narrow one, as narrow maybe as the window sill which is crucial to this case. But this is a criminal charge of gravity and, even though one may suspect that his *intention* was to commit the offence charged, unless the facts show with clarity that he in fact committed it he ought not to remain convicted . . .

We have to say that this appeal must be allowed and the conviction quashed.

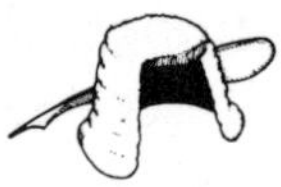

Two judges were fishing dry-fly upstream. So absorbed were they that they failed to notice how late it was. They were lost as darkness fell. In the distance was a faint light towards which they walked. They found a cottage, the door of which was opened by a beautiful young woman. She allowed them to use the phone and gave them each a dry sherry, and then another and a third. They accepted her invitation to dinner. She was a cordon bleu cook and the claret and port were of the very best. Eventually they deemed it prudent to accept an invitation to stay the night.

Exactly nine months later one judge phoned the other. 'George, you remember our fishing expedition and invitation to stay to dinner and then stay the night? Did you by any chance visit the lady's bedroom?' 'Yes, why?' 'Did you pretend you were me and give her my name?' 'Yes, I'm afraid I did. No trouble, I hope.' 'Well, she died three days ago and left me £100,000.'

*Pending Land Action*

*Undue influence*

An Irish defendant was in court charged with indecent exposure. Proceedings were severely hampered by constant interruptions from the defendant which were beginning to try the patience of the judge. Finally at the latest outburst of the defendant, the judge banged his hammer on the table and said 'Mr O'Reilly, any further interruptions from you will force me to clear the Court and hold the rest of the proceedings in camera'. O'Reilly replied 'To be sure, your Honour, to be sure, but what is this "in camera" business'? The judge wearily drew himself up from the bench and in a lordly fashion declared 'Counsel for the prosecution knows what "in camera" means, defending counsel knows what "in camera" means and most importantly I know what I mean. We will continue.' In due course O'Reilly took his turn in the witness box and gave his version of events thus: 'Well, your honour, it was a fine, fine morning and I was taking my lassie for a walk. I was feeling a bit frisky and so we went into the bushes and I was astrapping her away when this policeman' – 'Mr O'Reilly,' the judge interrupted, 'can you kindly explain to the court what this 'astrapping her away' means?'. 'Your honour, prosecuting Counsel knows what I mean, defending Counsel knows what I mean and if you had been there with your bloody camera, you would know what I mean'.

Many years ago I acted in the estate of a Latvian who had died in this country, appointing a fellow-countryman as his executor, and directing that his modest estate should be remitted in goods to relatives back in his homeland. His executor who spoke patchy English duly brought in all the necessary papers, but on being told the terms of the will he kept saying 'Why no pennies for me?'

After two or three further interviews, during which he repeated 'You no pennies for me – I no sign,' it had become patently obvious that we were getting nowhere. The alternatives were too horrendous to contemplate. Finally I had a blazing row with the executor telling him that he ought to be ashamed of himself in letting a fellow-countryman down and that it was his moral duty to carry out his wishes. This was then followed by a letter confirming the advice which had been forcefully given. As a last minute inspiration, knowing that many of the expatriate Russians and Latvians are practising Christians, I suggested to him that if he was in any doubt about his moral duties he should show the letter to his parish priest and follow his advice.

Some days later, much to the delight of the office staff who had heard the original noisy disagreement taking place, the executor returned resplendent in dog collar – he was the parish priest!

The lecture hall at the Inns of Court School of Law is cavernous and holds many hundreds of hopeful student barristers. The lecturers have their specialist fields and a particular style in delivering their hour-long papers.

One Monday morning, not so many years ago, a lecture on the law of evidence was being given by a guest lecturer, an academic of high standing who travelled weekly for the task from a certain fenland university. His manner was dry and thoroughly erudite. Perhaps too dry and too erudite for the first thing on a Monday.

On that day the students were spread loosely about the hall and after the lecture had been proceeding for some time a voice called from somewhere at the back of the hall 'Louder!'

The lecturer stopped. He looked up. He started again, speaking louder.

After five more minutes the same voice called out 'Slower!'

The lecturer stopped. He looked up and appeared a little irritated. He started again, speaking slower.

After the elapse of another ten minutes the voice called again:

'More int-eresting!'

This is an exchange between counsel and the judge in the course of mitigation on behalf of a defendant who was charged with possessing controlled drugs:

Counsel: 'Your Honour, he only took morphine once and he took it like snuff.'
Judge: 'That takes a bit of swallowing . . . not for him but for me.'
Counsel: 'Your Honour, that's as may be, but I am instructed that he is now trying to put it behind him.'

Opinions from counsel are not always what is expected and rarely what is hoped for. However, on one occasion, counsel produced for a solicitor an opinion that was clear, incisive and relevant. It was apparent that counsel had not only read the whole of the instructions but had even done much research himself and thoroughly mastered the circumstances of the case. This was so unusual an occurrence that the solicitor wrote back to counsel a letter which said merely,

'Dear Sir, Proverbs Chapter 8 Verse 14, yours faithfully . . .'

There was some delay before a reply was received because, counsel's chambers being what they are, it was some time before anyone recognised this as being a reference to the Bible. Chambers did not of course have one and they had to arrange for the junior to go out and steal one from the public library. When eventually the text was discovered, it read:

'Counsel is mine with sound wisdom, I have understanding, I gain strength.'

Eventually the reply was received:

'Dear Sir, Proverbs Chapter 8 Verse 17, Yours faithfully . . .'

This was checked, it was revealed to be:

'I love them that love me.'

And when sentencing an inebriate vagrant: 'Now I am going to discharge you conditionally and I hope never to see you again – except of course on purely social occasions.'

*'To writing to you . . . wishing you Merry Xmas . . . Five Guineas . . .'*

Court Martial. Charge: Telling an untruth to a superior officer. Orderly Officer inspecting guard finds the trumpeter without his trumpet and asks where it is. Drunken trumpeter replies 'Up my f——— arse'. Charge continues 'in that he when asked by 2/Lt R, where his trumpet was, replied "up my f——— arse" well knowing the same not to be true.'

The judge had had a bad morning. Counsel had been impertinent to him, the jury had acquitted a defendant who, the judge had told them, quite clearly, was guilty. Now there was another snivelling wretch before him, pleading guilty to a minor offence. 'You'll go to prison for three months!' thundered the judge. The clerk whispered timidly to him 'But it's only a £10 fine, Your Honour. 'AND you'll pay a fine of £10!' roared the judge.

A solicitor was acting for a young girl who had given birth to an illegitimate child and was asking the court to grant a maintenance order. The alleged father was denying paternity. The solicitor on behalf of the girl asked 'Did you take precautions before the act of intercourse?' The answer was, 'Yes, I made sure my parents were in bed first.'

*Lack of capacity*

*Adverse Possession*

A solicitor received a letter which said:

'Dear Sir,
I understand that you have been having an affair with my wife. I suggest that we meet on Wednesday next, the 15th at my office to discuss the matter.
Yours faithfully . . .'

The solicitor replied as follows:

'Dear Sir,
Thank you for your circular letter. I have no intention of attending a public meeting at your office next Wednesday.
Yours faithfully . . .'

The glorious ambiguity of the English language is illustrated by a story told by Mr Justice Millett. As a young Junior, he was sitting in a county court waiting for his own case to be reached and listening to the previous case, conducted by a solicitor. It was a small claim for the price of goods sold and delivered. The price had not been expressly agreed, but was the standard price charged by the plaintiff to all his customers. This meant that the plaintiff had to show that his prices were reasonable. The solicitor forgot to ask his client about this, so the judge intervened.

'Were your prices reasonable?' he asked the plaintiff.

'Oh, more than reasonable, your Honour,' the plaintiff replied.

*An Imminent Breach of Rule 3 of the Solicitors' Practice Rules 1936–72*

In November 1900, land was conveyed to three trustees without mention in the conveyance of any trust or purpose for which the property was conveyed. In 1932 the last surviving trustee appointed new trustees and acknowledged in the deed of appointment that the land, the subject of the original purchase, was to be disposed of and applied in accordance with secret trusts. He appointed three new trustees to act jointly with himself. The secret trusts were not revealed in any document. The last of the four trustees, realizing that it was necessary, appointed new trustees in 1967. The new trustees sought details from him of the secret trusts and were told that he had asked a like question on his appointment and was then told that, as the trusts were secret, it was not open to the appointing trustee to tell him what those secret trusts were. They remained a secret and still remain a secret.

In the event, with the consent of the Charity Commissioners, educational trusts were declared but the secret trusts remain undisclosed to this day.

An elderly lady, who had just been left by her husband after many years of marriage, consulted her solicitor. She explained that their relationship had become increasingly strained over the years, and describing the blazing row which had precipitated her husband's departure. The atmosphere had become so charged that the dog bit him as he stormed out of the room.

'And I'd have bitten him myself if I'd had my bottom set in' she commented.

A well-known petty criminal had been arrested on a charge of assault. The youth was detained overnight in the police cells pending a plea the following morning. He had been out drinking heavily, he was casually dressed and the police had taken all the usual precautions before placing him in the cells.

He was duly brought before the bench in the morning. He was wearing what was left of a T-shirt and a pair of ripped jeans, and obviously suffered from a monumental hangover. As the court was like a second home to him, he was not unduly impressed by his surroundings and was somewhat laconic in his replies to questions put to him. Whilst standing, he insisted on bunching his fists in his pockets. The young lady clerk became increasingly annoyed at his slovenly appearance and general demeanour, eventually snapping at him to remove his hands from his pockets.

The accused, with what in better circumstances might have amounted to a glint in his blood-stained eyes, suggested as politely as he could that this wouldn't be a good idea. Unfortunately, he overdid things by stating that the clerk would probably regret it if he did. Naturally, already irritated, she retorted that he would almost certainly regret it even more if he didn't. The accused looked at the clerk with what amounted to pity, removed his fists from his pockets and allowed his jeans to fall to the floor, revealing amongst other things that the T-shirt was the only other item of clothing he was wearing. The police, of course, had removed his belt the previous night.

One should always bear in mind that, however improbable it may seem, the client just may know what he's talking about!

*Incorporeal Hereditaments*

*Pre-completion Search*

A defendant was being tried for living on the immoral earnings of a girl who had managed to escape from him and had taken a respectable job as a shop assistant. A witness gave evidence that the defendant had visited the shop and demanded money.

Defendant's counsel: 'I put it to you that you misheard him. He did not ask for money. He asked for honey.'

Witness: 'At the bacon counter?'

An out-of-town solicitor involved in a case at Selby Magistrates Court was trying to explain to the magistrates his client's careless driving. Having difficulty doing this and obviously short of things to say, he fumbled verbally for a short while and then announced 'He may in fact have slightly fallen asleep'.

In my first case in the High Court I appeared for the plaintiff. I was addressing the judge, Baillache J., in my final speech when he rebuked me.

I was very hurt and said to him. 'I was only repeating to your Lordship something your Lordship said a short time ago.'

The judge looked at me and said, 'Mr Weitzman, if I say something foolish, you should not repeat it.'

The newly-qualified solicitor was due to make his first appearance in open court. He was understandably somewhat nervous, particularly as the judge was known to have a sharp tongue. He had prepared his case thoroughly and had dressed for the occasion, but had of course borrowed the robes kept in the office for such county court cases.

The plaintiff's solicitor duly opened the case and everything proceeded smoothly, right up to the point where our hero had to say his first words. In his excitement, he didn't realise that he was standing on the hem of his gown which was several sizes too large for him. He took his cue, jumped to his feet and opened his mouth to speak. He had got as far as 'Your Hon . . .' when he heard a rather loud ripping sound and felt his leg apparently going into spasm. He very hurriedly sat down to sort himself out, at which point the judge removed his glasses, looked at the seated solicitor rather quizzically and said 'Well, Mr Smith, that may be the shortest opening address on record, but I doubt if it helps your client. Do you wish to try again?'

God and the Devil were arguing over the responsibility for repair concerning the fence separating Heaven and Hell. The dispute could not be settled and God told the Devil that he intended to consult his solicitor on the matter. The Devil retorted – 'And where would you expect to find a solicitor?'

A Yorkshire farmer, suing for damages for delivery of bad hay, insisted upon handing up to the judge a sample of the offending crop. His opponent began to laugh, whereupon the judge asked him what was causing such amusement. 'Well,' he replied, 'I have heard the law called an ass, Your Honour, but I have never before seen anyone try to feed it.'

When I first arrived in Fiji as a Crown Counsel I was introduced to a well known character called Bagnall who had held various magisterial and judicial posts. He impressed all by a robust practical approach and in particular by his insistence on 'views' when the entire court went to the actual scene of an offence since this often served to confirm oral evidence. When he sat on the Court of Appeal this was not possible because such courts do not, except in exceptional circumstances, have witnesses testify before them but rely on transcripts of proceedings in the court below. One appeal related to a case of rape committed in an hotel room and there had been an eye witness, a chamber maid, who watched through the key hole. Mr Justice Bagnall enquired as to whether or not measurements had been taken of the key hole and whether or not there had been any check as to the view through it. When counsel told him that this had not been done, he burst out 'Why, had I been the trial judge, without question nothing would have satisfied me unless we had all gone to the room and I had looked through the key hole and had the whole scene re-enacted before my very eyes!'

*The Saga of Arnold W. Cattermole (or Unrequieted Love)*

It was not the thing that happened
At solicitors Futtock and Quirk,
But in a musty corner there
A quiet passion lurked,
Nurtured in the bosom of a humble lawyer's clerk.
To Arnold W. Cattermole
Love was not a lark.

The object of his passion was
A dolly little miss.
She was a shorthand typist in
The room just down from his.
She'd set the fires a' burning
About two months before,
By blowing a kiss and smiling
When he came through the door.

The typists all thought Arnold was
A funny sort of bloke.
They'd egged on Arnie's fancy;
They did it as a joke.
But Arnold only realised
His cup was running o'er;
His heart was filled with wondrous love.
The problem – how to show her.

Then Arnold and his heart's desire
Were both sent to a meeting,
And Arnold thought – now here's my chance;
His heart was loudly beating.
The two of them sat side by side
On the returning train,

'Isabella' Arnold said
(For that was the maiden's name)

'You might call this a local search,
Enquiries on my part
To see if you'll an easement grant
Upon my aching heart.

I see us now by covenants
Both mutually bound.'
With that he moved up closer and
Put his arm around her waist and
Held her in fee simple.
'Just like a High Court seal,' he said,
'On each charming cheek a dimple.'

I'm raising requisitions on the title
to your hand.
Are there any restrictions, stipulations?'
She said 'I'm not a bit of land.
And further, Mr Cattermole,
take your hand from off my knee.
My boyfriend has prescriptive rights,
In fact, he lives with me.

He's also of the jealous type, and
Won't welcome a third party.
He's a seventh dan at Judo
And a blackbelt at Karate.'

Next day at the office with
Tear-sodden handkerchief
Sat Arnold with his head in hands
Beside himself with grief.
Then suddenly he calmed himself
And to his task he bent

And drafted Arnold Cattermole's
Last will and testament.

They found him shortly after lunch,
On his face, death's twisted smile;
He'd thrown himself from the very top
Of his largest current file.

When I was inspecting a house in the Yorkshire Dales the occupant informed me she was eighty-seven years of age. Upon taking leave of her I commented it was very doubtful whether I would live to be her age.

'How old are you now lad?' she enquired.

'Fifty-seven,' was my reply.

'No, I don't think you will,' she confidently responded, accompanied by an astute appraisal of my appearance.

It is the new barrister's first day in the High Court, representing the respondent in a family matter. The whiteness of his wig almost dazzles his wily seen-it-all opponent as the latter rises to address the judge. 'M'Lord,' he thunders, 'I apply for the usual order' and with that thumps back down onto his seat. But his one-upmanship meets its match as the younger man shows his mettle: 'And I, M'Lord, object,' counters he, 'for the usual reasons.'

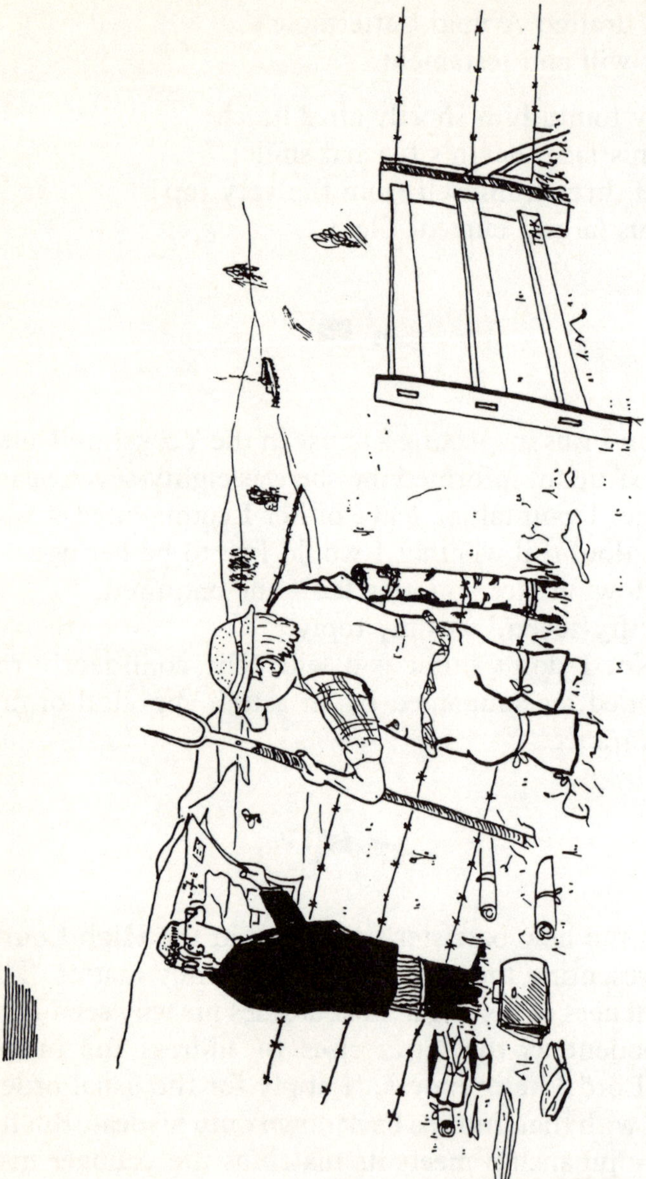

'. . . the green bits are the grass, sir . . .'

'. . . part of the problem is that it's based on English law . . .'

In his life of Sir Edward Marshall Hall, Marjoribanks recites the allegedly true story of one of his hero's early cases. Hall appeared in a magistrates court in a paternity case. He was convinced he had satisfied the bench that his client was not the father of the illegitimate child. However, the bench decided that his client was the father of the child and he was ordered to pay so much a week accordingly. After the case, Marshall Hall, who knew one of the magistrates, happened to have a drink with him. 'You know sir,' said the young barrister, 'I can't see how you came to the decision that my client was the father of that child.' 'Well', said the magistrate, 'on your arguments we agreed with you but when we saw your client sitting next to you and when we looked at the child we realised that he must be the father'. 'What?' said the future silk. 'That wasn't my client, that was my clerk.'

*Custody – The Pennine Way*

The law is ever-changing. New phrases emerge overnight and the judge must know them all. Borstal has now become Youth Custody but a judge tired of change recently imposed the following sentence on a nineteen-year-old yobbo, intending to reflect the Court's serious displeasure at his behaviour:

'So you, young man, must be dealt with harshly, to set an example to others and to deter them. For these offences the only proper sentence is one of 12 months' . . . Youth Hostelling.'

A judge of the old 'blood and thunder' type duly convicted a particularly defiant rogue who had been contemptuous of the whole court proceedings. The irritated judge continued:

'Moreover, if you do not repent you will surely go to Hell where there will be nothing but fornication, gambling, drinking and loose women'. From the back of the court a voice came 'Oh death, where is thy sting?'

A solicitors' cashier presented to one of the partners for signature a crossed cheque drawn payable to 'St. Michael and All Angels', which moved the partner to break into verse, thus:

Pay 'St Michael and All Angels' the payee was plain,
But thought chased thought around my fertile brain,
The cheque is crossed, the usual rule applies,
But are there Banks in far celestial skies?
'A/C payee', but what a joint account,
All Angels is an infinite amount
Of signatories, but at what Bank on high,
Which one deserves a branch up in the sky,
Which behind the pearly gates, so glistening,
Could it be the one that's always listening.
Has the Deity been too impressed
By all those adverts from Nat West.
Then there's Barclays too, and Lloyds of course,
But no, the Devil's more akin to that black horse,
I think the T.S.B. the angels bless,
After all, it is the one that likes to answer 'Yes'!

Counsel: 'Among the property stolen was a record player.'

Judge: 'Is that what in my youth I used to call a gramophone?'

Counsel: 'In your youth, Your Honour, I believe you will have called it a phonograph.'

It is easy for an advocate to assume that witnesses will have the same logical approach to the evidence that the advocate has. In a case of driving without due care and attention the defendant had turned right just as the vehicle behind was in the act of overtaking him. He was being cross examined by the prosecuting solicitor.

Solicitor: 'Did you look in your rear mirror before turning right?'

Defendant: 'Yes.'

Solicitor: 'Did you see the car overtaking you?'

Defendant: 'No.'

Solicitor: 'Are you saying that the other car was in your blind spot?'

Defendant: 'Er, yes.'

Solicitor: 'But your car is equipped with wing mirrors and these wing mirrors do away with the blind spot, don't they?'

Defendant: 'Er, yes – er, sometimes.'

Solicitor: 'Why only sometimes?'

Defendant: 'Why only sometimes what?'

Solicitor: 'Do away with those blind spots.'

Defendant: 'What blind spots?'

Collapse of prosecuting solicitor.

*'. . . It's up to you, but I wouldn't speak for too long . . .'*

The attractive young blond girl who had applied for a maintenance order was giving evidence, on oath, of her means. She had explained to the magistrates that she was unemployed and in receipt only of state benefits and the magistrates proceeded to question her about her expenses.

'Do you pay a mortgage?'

'No.'

'Rent?'

'No, I live with my parents.'

'Board?'

'No, not really, I try to get out at least one or two nights every week.'

Mr G., a Bradford wool merchant, was very successful in business and became a millionaire. He was approached by a young engineer and agreed to lend him £2,000 to develop an invention. The borrower, instead of using the money as agreed, spent the money on wine and women. When the forthright Yorkshireman found out he pursued the borrower in the Courts.

Mr. Justice Scrutton was trying the case. Mr. G. was in the witness box and his counsel said, 'What did you do when you found this matter out?' Mr. G. replied, 'I went to him and said "I've found you out".' 'No! No!' said counsel, 'What were the exact words you used on that occasion?' Mr. G. replied 'I've found you out, you bugger. I've got you by the balls.' Mr. Justice Scrutton then remarked, 'And if I may be allowed to say so, Mr. G. – a very commanding position in which to be.'

A deserting husband was summonsed in the Magistrates Court for being two years in arrears with his wife's maintenance. He stated that he was a smallholder living in a small back-to-back dwelling with no furniture whatsoever, the Bailiffs having taken it; he had nothing on his smallholding, as he had no money to cultivate it; his chicken coop was empty, he having eaten the last chicken; he had failed to pay forty-seven different County Court debts at rates varying from 5p to 75p per month; he had no work and no prospects of any work; electricity had been cut off and he was six months in arrears with his rent.

After this sorry story he was asked by the wife's solicitor: 'Why do you not want to pay your wife any maintenance?'

The deserting husband turned to the magistrates and said: 'It's like giving oats to a dead 'orse.'

It was nearing the end of term and in the High Court a testy old judge was sitting in the Queen's Bench Division. He had been listening with growing impatience to a well known silk make his submissions which seemed to that judge both repetitive and interminable. He leaned forward and said in a forthright tone:

'It is all very well, Mr So-and-So, but what you say is going in here . . .' he pointed to his left ear, '. . . and out of here,' and pointed to his right.

'But my Lord,' said that wise silk, 'what is there to prevent it?'

Counsel for the petitioner in dissolution proceedings: 'M'lord, the petitioner and the respondent have been married for seven years during which period he has only spoken to her six times – and there are six children of the marriage.

In a personal injuries claim it was alleged by the plaintiff that as a result of the accident he was unable to raise his right arm above shoulder height. It was suspected by the defendant's advisers that the allegation was bogus.

Counsel for the defendants rose to cross-examine the plaintiff. 'Show us how high you can raise your arm,' he said. Gingerly the plaintiff raised his arm to a horizontal position. 'Thank you,' said counsel and the plaintiff lowered his arm. 'Now show me how high you could raise it before the accident,' said counsel. Immediately the plaintiff, zealous to demonstrate the difference, shot up his arm, only to collapse in mortification as he realised that that was the end of his case.

A judge once began a summing-up as follows:

'Members of the Jury, one of my functions is to help you understand the issues in this trial more clearly. Now the charge is theft by which I mean burglary or should I say attempted burglary.'

*Mens Rea*

*Actus Rea*

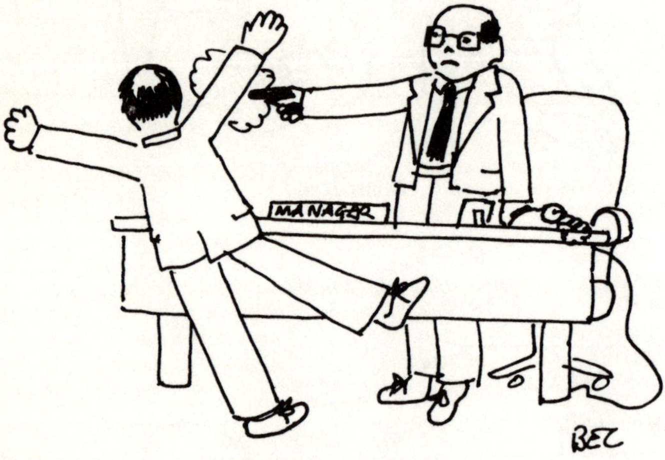


*Constructive Dismissal*

An assiduous young solicitor had a client whose defence was hopeless in the face of overwhelming prosecution evidence. Undeterred, he took long and comprehensive instructions and briefed the ablest barrister he knew. Come the trial, his client was revealed in the witness box for the rogue he undoubtedly was and was bailed to await the following and final day of his case. Fearing the worst he failed to appear in the morning and therefore missed his counsel's brilliant address to the jury which resulted in his aquittal.

The young solicitor was beside himself with pride and sent telegrams, for this was some time ago, to all his client's possible addresses in these terms:

'Justice has triumphed.'

A day later he himself received a telegram: 'Appeal at once.'

Soon after my call to the Bar I received my first brief. It was at the Tottenham Magistrates Court, to defend a butcher's boy charged with indecent assault on a girl. The allegation was that he had placed her hand on his private parts.

I was cross-examining and put to the girl that she was wrong, that he was carrying a parcel of sausages and put her hand on one of the sausages.

She looked at me with scorn and said 'Have you ever seen a sausage with a throb in it?'

The boy was bound over to keep the peace.

A solicitor was instructed to prepare a will for a local businessman. After providing for various pecuniary legacies the testator continued:

> 'I instruct my Executor to obtain a Lemon, to cut it into two halves and to send one half to Her Majesty's Inspector of Taxes and the other half to Her Majesty's Collector of Taxes in each case with the message the message "Now squeeze this".'

The solicitor was appointed executor. When in due course the testator died he carried out his wishes exactly as instructed. Although neither the Inspector of Taxes or the Collector of Taxes responded officially, both were highly amused by the originality of the testator's direction.

A 'lady of the streets' was appearing on a charge under the Vagrancy Act and she duly entered the dock. The Clerk to the Justices called out her name and read over the charge saying 'You are Patricia . . . and you are charged as follows in that you, a common prostitute, did on the . . . day of . . . at Rouen Road within this City importune etc . . .' The defendant immediately shouted an objection. The clerk asked her what was her objection about. She replied 'I refuse to be described in this insulting manner.' She objected to the use of the term 'common prostitute'. The clerk very politely asked her how she would prefer to be described. 'I would like to be called a Lady Solicitor, the same as that young woman who is sitting down there,' she replied, pointing to a newly qualified and blushing female sitting at the solicitors' table!

*'Felix qui potuit rerum cognoscere causas': Virgil,* Georgics *ii, 490. (Happy is the man who knows the causes of things.)*

An ignorant, petty pickpocket was charged with stealing a watch. He had the good fortune to be defended by an excellent barrister, whose eloquence on behalf of his client succeeded in obtaining an acquittal. On being informed he had been acquitted, his immediate question was 'Does that mean I have to give the watch back?'

A farmer was on trial for rape. He had caught the girl picking apples in his orchard. He decided to defend himself in court and cross examined the girl thus:

'Caught you picking apples, didn't I?'

'Yes.'

'Not for the first time.'

'No.'

'When I caught you before I told you what I would do if I caught you again.'

'Yes.'

'And that was what I did to you, wasn't it?'

'Yes.'

The judge now intervened and dismissed the case in that the girl had gone to the orchard knowing what would happen and therefore was consenting. The judge however turned to the defendant and said, 'Don't go on threatening girls like this otherwise you will have no apples left in your orchard.'

Advocacy is a simple matter of sincerity. Once you have learned to fake that, the rest is easy.

The minority shareholders in a small company complained that for many years they had not been sent notices of the Annual General Meetings, as the Articles of Association required. The Secretary of the company was giving evidence. Cross-examining him, counsel asked:

'Why, in 1958, did you not send a notice of the Annual General Meeting to Mr X?'

'Because,' replied the Secretary, 'Mr X had died without leaving a forwarding address.'

A young and rather inexperienced barrister was briefed for one of the parties in a case, where two ships had collided. The Master of the ship, whose owners he represented, was a salty and rugged character but not very bright. The young barrister carefully asked him all the necessary questions leading up to the collision and then the following exchange occurred:

Counsel: 'When it became evident that catastrophe was imminent, what sensation did that arouse in your consciousness?'
Witness: 'Eh?'
Judge: 'He means what did you think when you saw you were going to hit the other ship.'
Witness: 'Aargh – you could have buggered me through me oilskins.'
Counsel (nonplussed): 'I beg your pardon.'
Judge (always helpful!): 'He must mean that he was taken aback.'

Moral, never ask one question too many.

*Dependent Relative Revocation*

*A Trustee carrying out a Chesterfield Apportionment*

A letter sent by one solicitor to another solicitor from whom he was awaiting a Contract in connection with the sale of property, read as follows:

'Dear Sirs,
Re: Our client – Mr. X.
Re: Your client – Mr. Y.
Re: Property ABC Street.
St. Matthew 11, Verse 3.
Yours faithfully,'

Chapter 11, Verse 3 reads 'And said unto him, Art thou he that should come, or do we look for another?'

Dewsbury Magistrates' Court (1983): Prosecutor to Bench: 'I appear for the prosecution and my friend Mr C . . . appears for the money.'

A solicitor and his young assistant visited a lady octagenarian client for whom they had prepared a will. Before asking the client to sign the will the solicitor was reading it aloud to her to ensure it accorded with her instructions. She listened carefully to a not inconsiderable list of specific bequests to different charities and, obviously becoming anxious as the list of gifts grew, stopped the solicitor and asked 'But will there be enough left over for me?'. It was only after some tactful explaining that he was allowed to carry on.

A young mother was using the family minibus to drive her own children, and those of various neighbours, to school one morning. Being late, she drove faster than the law allowed, and was flagged down by a police patrolman, who came over to her, looked in the back of the minibus and said to her, ''Ello, 'Ello, Madam, you've been going a bit over the limit, haven't you?' To which the lady replied, 'I'm sorry, constable – but they're not all mine!'

Farmer plaintiff, suing for damages suffered by his Yorkshire Dales land being flooded as a result of his neighbour diverting a stream:
'Nowt will grow there now. I have tried every darned crop I can think of and nothing works. I have even tried leeks because they sounded right but nowt works. I'm at a loss to know what to plant next.'

Judge: 'Have you tried rice?'

An old man, whose garments had served far longer than they were ever designed to do, and whose personal hygiene was not of the highest order, came into the office seeking a small loan. His modest interest under a family trust was already seriously overdrawn, so his request was initially refused.

'You can have these as security', he persisted, placing his false teeth on the table. He got his loan and happily redeemed his pledge several weeks later.

*A Partner giving notice of Intention to Dissolve*

I was briefed to appear on behalf of two Jewish girls, who were crossing Regent Street and were knocked down and slightly injured, in a civil case before His Honour Judge Cluer at the Whitechapel County Court.

The jury retired to consider the evidence, and returned to the Court. The foreman was asked by the judge 'How do you find?'

The foreman, who was Jewish, stroked his long beard, took up his note and read out 'We find for the plaintiff Becky Cohen for £50 with costs. We find for the plaintiff Rachel Levy for £20 with costs. We say it was a pure accident and exonerate the driver from all blame.'

A police officer's statement in an excess alcohol case read as follows:

P.C. Jones was proceeding in his police vehicle along Talbot Road Stretford when he saw a Morris motor car veering from the crown of the road towards the curb and back. He caused the vehicle to stop and spoke to the driver who was, in fact, the defendant. He noticed that the defendant's breath smelled strongly of alcohol, that his eyes were glazed and his speech was slurred. Accordingly P.C. Jones requested that the defendant supply a specimen of breath on the breathalyser device whereupon the defendant thrust a tray of fish and chips into the face of P.C. Jones saying 'F—— off ——'. P.C. Jones took this as a refusal.

*Codes of Conduct*

*Rule No. 1 An advocate is an officer of the court and will conduct himself with dignity and decorum at all times in court.*

*This rule forbids not only the obvious, thus . . .*

*but also . . . any conduct likely to distract the court or an opponent from the business in hand.*

*Objections, when taken, should be accompanied by at least ordinary courtesy.*

*Cheating or sharp practice of any description is out of the question.*

A four-year-old-girl had been indecently assaulted by a man. As a Prosecuting Solicitor at Strangeways Magistrates Court, I was reading the record of the interview between the child and a policewoman. The interview was in question and answer form with a variety of childish terms being employed for the various parts of the female and male anatomy. The final question from the policewoman was 'Could you tell us what this man looked like?' to which the alleged reply from the four-year-old was 'Yes, I would describe him as being 5′ 9″ tall and of stocky build.'

The young advocate had just come out of court. He had defended his client, unsuccessfully, for drinking after hours. He turned to his client and said 'Well, Henry, sorry about that, but £2 is not bad.'

Henry replied, 'Don't worry about it, lad. I knew I had no chance as soon as I saw my cousin was the Chairman.'

A defendant in the Crown Court had been found guilty. The judge announced that, in view of the way the offence had been committed, he intended to impose the maximum sentence the law allowed: two years imprisonment.

The defendant was heard to say 'I can do that standing on my head.' The judge added 'I will sentence you to a further six months for contempt of court, and to give you time to get back on your feet again.'

I was addressing a jury and I picked out the member who appeared to be most intelligent. I addressed him particularly, hoping he would influence his fellow-members.

To my horror, I discovered later he was deaf and had not heard a word I said.

In the early 1950s, Sir John Senter QC was the doyen of the tax Bar. One afternoon he addressed the House of Lords, and found that his argument was not well received. Overnight, however, he thought of a new point, which he convinced himself would save the day. Next morning, he told their Lordships that he had a new point, and proceeded to outline it to them. No sooner had he done so than Lord Morton of Henryton intervened, and in two short sentences completely demolished the argument. Sir John Senter was crestfallen. Ruefully, he told their Lordships:

'When I thought of that point last night, I felt like stout Cortez when he first gazed on the Pacific.'

Lord Morton cut him short with the devastating observation: 'But surely, Sir John, when stout Cortez first gazed on the Pacific he remained silent?'

Another sentence is sometimes attributed to Judge Maude, also dealing with an inebriated vagrant: 'You must serve fourteen days and if you take my advice when you are released you will never touch alcohol again – not even a teeny weeny sherry.'

*Rule No. 2 An advocate must accept instructions when properly tendered and accompanied by a reasonable fee.*

*There are of course exceptions to this.*

*An advocate is an advocate twenty four hours each day and must never allow himself to forget this.*

*Rule No. 3 An advocate may not advertise his services or otherwise tout for business.*

*There are of course many ways of advertising and unless this rule is observed in the spirit rather than the letter . . . . .*

. . . . . *strange results can ensue.*

On September 4, 1967, at Willesden magistrates' court the appellant, Vincent Martel Fagan, was convicted of assaulting David Morris, a constable of the Metropolitan Police Force, on August 31, 1967, when in the execution of his duty. The appellant appealed to the Middlesex Quarter Sessions.

The following facts were either proved or admitted: P.C. David Morris was at all material times in the execution of his duty; on August 31, 1967, the appellant drove a motor vehicle in Fortunegate Road, London, N.W. 10 near the junction with Craven Park Road, London, N.W.10. While the appellant was in the course of reversing his motor vehicle from the said road on to a pedestrian crossing in Craven Park Road, P.C. David Morris asked the appellant to pull into the said road against the north kerb so that he could ask the appellant to produce documents relating to the appellant's driving. First of all the vehicle stopped and it did not move. P.C. David Morris, who had walked into the middle of the said road, pointed out to the appellant a suitable parking place against the kerb of the said road. The appellant drove the vehicle toward P.C. David Morris and stopped it with its near side a substantial distance from the kerb. P.C. David Morris went up to the appellant and asked him to park the vehicle closer to the kerb. P.C. David Morris walked to a position about one yard in front of the vehicle and pointed to the exact position against the kerb. The appellant drove the vehicle in the direction of P.C. David Morris and stopped it with its front offside wheel on P.C. David Morris's left foot. P.C. David

Morris said to the appellant, 'Get off, you are on my foot'. The appellant's driving window was open. The appellant said, 'F—— you, you can wait.' The appellant then turned off the ignition, or at least the engine stopped running. P.C. David Morris then said to the appellant several times, 'Get off my foot.' The appellant then said very reluctantly, 'Okay man, okay.' The appellant thereafter very slowly turned on the ignition and reversed the vehicle off P.C. David Morris's foot. As a result of the appellant's act of omission P.C. David Morris's left big toe was injured. The toe was swollen and slightly bruised . . .

On the facts stated above, the deputy chairman and the justices were left in doubt whether the initial mounting of the motor wheel on P.C. David Morris's foot was intentional on the part of the appellant or accidental. They were satisfied beyond all reasonable doubt that the appellant knowingly, provocatively and unnecessarily allowed the motor wheel to remain on P.C. David Morris's foot after P.C. David Morris said, 'Get off, you are on my foot' . . . The deputy chairman and the justices came to the conclusion that the charge of assault on P.C. David Morris had been made out, and dismissed the appeal.

The village band came to a fork in the road. The band went to the left but the bass drummer, oblivious to all but his drumming, went to the right. An urchin ran after him, shouting, 'Mister, Mister, t'band's gone t'other way.'

'That's all reet, lad,' replied the drummer. 'Ah knows tune.'

The prosecution allegation, in a misleading trade description case in India, was that the defendant had sold locally distilled whisky, under the evocative name of 'Highland Laddie', or 'Cock o' the North', claiming that it was made in Scotland – the very words which appeared at the foot of the decorative label on the bottle.

'Quite true,' said the defendant, 'the labels were indeed made in Scotland.'

Case dismissed.

A very young defence counsel, called Mr Bury, found himself for the first time before a rather crotchety judge at the assizes. The judge asked him his name.

'My name is Bury, my Lord.'

'How do you spell that?'

'B-U-R-Y, my Lord.'

'Ah, you mean "Berry".'

'It is pronounced "Bury" my Lord.'

'Nonsense, I shall call you "Berry".'

On the second day of the trial prosecuting counsel was on his feet when the judge interrupted him.

'Just a moment, what is so funny, Mr Berry?'

'Nothing, my Lord.'

'Balderdash, I insist on your explaining what you find so amusing.'

'Well, my Lord, I was sitting here looking at the members of the jury, and thinking, they believe they are sitting on a jury, whereas your Lordship and I know better.'

During submissions in a rape case a judge intervened with the following singular observation:

'Basically there are two kinds of rape as I well know from trying them both.'

*Legal Hierarchy*

*Senior Partner*

Leaps tall buildings in a single bound,
Is more powerful than a locomotive,
Is faster than a speeding bullet,
Walks on water,
Gives policy to God.

*Junior partner*

Leaps short buildings in a single bound,
Is more powerful than a switch engine,
Is just as fast as a speeding bullet,
Walks on water if the sea is calm,
Talks with God.

*Associate*

Leaps short buildings with a running start and a favourable wind,
Is almost as powerful as a switch engine,
Is faster than a speeding bike,
Walks on water in a swimming pool,
Talks with God if special request is approved.

*Managing Clerk*

Clears a wooden hut,
Loses race with locomotive,
Can fire a speeding bullet,
Swims well,
Is occasionally addressed by God.

*Articled Clerk*

Runs into small buildings,
Recognizes locomotives two out of three times,
Shoots himself with a water pistol,
Dog paddles,
Mumbles to animals.

*Legal Secretary*

Lifts buildings to walk under,
Kicks locomotives off the tracks,
Catches speeding bullets in her teeth,
Freezes water with a single glance,
She IS God.

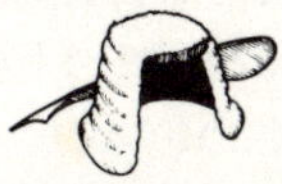

Counsel are occasionally guilty of opening their mouths before they put their brains in gear. This is a classic example:

The defendant was a sailor who on arrival home had been faced with overwhelming problems and resorted to crime. Counsel commenced his mitigation:

'Your Honour, having finally come on to dry land the defendant was totally at sea.'

There was a case in Singapore where a vessel had been scuttled. This is always difficult to prove directly but on this occasion the truth was blurted out by the cook in cross-examination:

Q. 'What time do you usually get up to make the crew's breakfast?'
A. '4.30.'
Q. 'What time did you get up on the day of the casualty?'
A. '3.30'
Q. 'Why was that?'
A. 'Had to cook big breakfast. Master said we were going to have long day in the boats.'

A senior judge in Ireland, not known for his sympathetic handling of those before him, is trying a case where the defence counsel is examining a prosecution witness. As soon as he asks a particular question the judge rules this inadmissible. Defence counsel then says there was a Queens Bench Division case which allowed a similar line of questioning. The judge immediately snaps 'It is still inadmissible as this court is not bound by Queens Bench Division.' Counsel replies that the case went to the Court of Appeal. The judge loudly declares that he is not bound by the Court of Appeal either. Counsel very respectfully points out that in fact there was a further appeal to the House of Lords. At this point the judge patiently said 'Oh, very well, ask your damn question,' to which counsel replied, 'It doesn't matter, it was of no consequence.'